# NURTURING BRILLIANCE IN GIFTED CHILDREN

## PROVEN STRATEGIES AND PRACTICAL TIPS TO UNLOCK POTENTIAL, PROMOTE EMOTIONAL RESILIENCE, AND NAVIGATE EDUCATIONAL SYSTEMS FOR LIFELONG SUCCESS

### WILLIAM J. CALLAGHAN

# CONTENTS

# INTRODUCTION

When Sarah first noticed her daughter, Emily, reading chapter books at the age of four, she was elated and overwhelmed. Emily's curiosity knew no bounds, and she asked questions about the universe that left Sarah scrambling for answers. However, along with her intellectual gifts came intense emotions and perfectionism. Emily would dissolve into tears at the slightest mistake in her math homework, and the traditional school system seemed ill-equipped to oversee her unique needs.

Sarah's story is not unique. Many parents of gifted children find themselves in a comparable situation, facing a blend of joy and challenges. These children often exhibit remarkable abilities, but they also come with emotional intensity, a heightened sense of perfectionism, and a set of educational needs that can be difficult to manage. These challenges can leave parents feeling isolated and unsure how best to support their children.

This book exists to be your guide through this journey. It aims to unlock your gifted child's potential, nurture their emotional resilience, and help you traverse educational systems for lifelong success. Drawing on insights from teachers, parents, and academic research, this book provides actionable strategies and relatable examples to help you raise your gifted child successfully.

What sets this book apart is its unique approach. While many resources focus solely on the intellectual development of gifted children, this book combines expert insights, practical advice, real-life examples, and case studies. This comprehensive guide is designed to be relatable and actionable, ensuring you have the tools to support your child in every aspect of their development.

My passion for helping parents of gifted children stems from personal and professional experiences. As a parent, I have faced many of the challenges discussed in this book. My child, like Emily, displayed exceptional abilities from an early age, and I found myself going through many emotional and educational hurdles. Professionally, I have spent many years researching gifted education and working with families to develop effective strategies.

This book's structure is designed to guide you through each stage of your child's development. The first section focuses on understanding giftedness, including identifying signs and understanding gifted children's emotional and social needs. The second section explores practical strategies for creating emotional resilience, managing perfectionism, and supporting your child's intellectual growth. The third section explores navigating educational systems, including advocating for your child's needs and finding the right academic environment. The book concludes with a section on life-long success, offering tips for preparing your child for adulthood and helping them develop a sense of purpose and fulfillment.

By reading this book, you will gain practical strategies you can implement immediately. You will find emotional support and encouragement, knowing you are not alone. Most importantly, you will be better equipped to help your child thrive academically and emotionally, setting them up for lifelong success.

I invite you to join me on this journey. Engage with the content, apply the strategies, and find hope and inspiration in your parenting journey. Together, we can address the challenges and joys of raising a gifted child, unlocking their potential, and creating emotional resilience.

# 1

# UNDERSTANDING YOUR GIFTED CHILD

You know that moment when your child asks you, "Why is the sky blue?" and you give a simple answer, only to be met with a follow-up question about Rayleigh scattering? Welcome to the club of parents raising gifted children. You are not alone in maneuvering through the beautiful chaos of intellectual curiosity, emotional intensity, and the sometimes-daunting task of finding the right educational fit. This chapter aims to demystify the many faces of giftedness, providing you with a clear understanding of what it means and how it manifests in diverse ways.

## 1.1 THE MANY FACES OF GIFTEDNESS

Giftedness is like a multifaceted gem—each face reflecting a different brilliance. It is not confined to academic prowess. Your child might solve complex math problems before they can tie their shoes, but that is just one side of the story. Intellectual giftedness often involves a high IQ and advanced critical thinking skills. These kids might breeze through school assignments, leaving their peers and sometimes even their teachers scratching their heads.

However, don't let their intellect overshadow other forms of giftedness.

Creative giftedness is another dazzling facet. These children think freely, creating innovative ideas and creative artifacts that can leave you in awe. They might be drawing intricate designs before they can spell their names. Leadership giftedness is just as fascinating. These kids have a knack for influencing others, displaying strong people skills and a natural ability to lead. For instance, they might organize their playmates into a small army for a backyard expedition!

Then there's psychomotor giftedness, where exceptional physical abilities come into play. Picture a young gymnast executing flips and twists that defy gravity or a budding athlete showing prowess in multiple sports. These children might need extra physical outlets to channel their abundant energy.

Giftedness can be revealed in various domains. Verbal-linguistic abilities, for example, might manifest as early reading and a vocabulary that can rival that of some adults. Logical-mathematical skills are evident in kids who quickly tackle complex calculations and logical reasoning. Spatial abilities shine in those who excel at visualization, creating masterpieces with building blocks, or solving puzzles with impressive speed.

Certain common traits often accompany these abilities. Curiosity is a hallmark. Gifted children ask relentless questions, diving deeply into subjects that capture their interest. Their intensity can be both a blessing and a challenge. They engage passionately with their interests, displaying high energy levels that can sometimes be exhausting to keep up with. Sensitivity is another frequent trait. These kids often have heightened emotional responses and a keen sense of empathy, which can make them acutely aware of how others feel.

However, misconceptions about giftedness abound. One of the most persistent myths is that gifted children are consistently high achievers. The reality is more nuanced. Giftedness does not guarantee success. Some talented children might need help academically and if their needs aren't met, it may lead to underachievement. They might become bored and disengaged in a traditional classroom that does not challenge them.

Another misconception is that giftedness is a one-size-fits-all label. In reality, it encompasses a broad spectrum of abilities and traits. Understanding this spectrum is necessary if you want to provide the proper support for your child. Remember, gifted children are individuals with unique strengths and challenges. By recognizing and nurturing their diverse abilities, you can help them thrive academically, emotionally, and socially.

Giftedness is a complex and multifaceted phenomenon. It can be intellectually stimulating and emotionally overwhelming for both the child and the parents. However, armed with the proper knowledge and strategies, you can help this child succeed in all aspects of life with confidence and grace.

## 1.2 ASYNCHRONOUS DEVELOPMENT: INTELLECTUAL VS. EMOTIONAL GROWTH

Imagine your child mastering algebra at age eight but throwing a tantrum because their favorite cartoon is not on. This is the essence of asynchronous development. Gifted children often develop intellectually at a pace that outstrips their emotional and physical growth. It is as if their brains are racing ahead while their hearts and social skills are taking their sweet time to catch up. They might quickly solve complex problems yet struggle to manage their emotions when things fail. This discrepancy can be overwhelming for parents and educators alike. One moment, the kid is a mini-Einstein: the next, they're an upset toddler.

This mismatch can create significant challenges, especially in social settings. While your child might be able to discuss quantum physics with an adult, they might need help connecting with their age-mates. Finding friends who share their interests and can keep up with their intellectual conversations is challenging. This often leads to potential social isolation. Your child might feel like they do not fit in, causing them to withdraw or act out. It is heartbreaking to watch them struggle to find their tribe, especially when many of them are so eager to connect.

To mitigate these challenges, parents can take several initiative-taking steps. Encouraging age-appropriate social activities is vital. While it is tempting to push them toward older kids who match their intellectual level, it is equally important to help them build relationships with peers their age. Activities like sports, arts, and group games can provide common ground that transcends intellectual differences. Providing emotional support and validation is also crucial. Acknowledging their feelings and helping them navigate their emotional landscape can make a substantial difference. Sometimes, all they need is to know that it is okay to feel out of sync.

Introducing intellectual peers through special programs or clubs can be a meaningful change. Programs designed for gifted children can offer a sense of belonging and understanding that is hard to find elsewhere. Whether it is a math club, a science camp, or a creative writing workshop, these environments allow them to thrive intellectually while connecting with like-minded individuals. These interactions can be a balm for their social struggles, providing a space where they feel seen and understood.

Take, for example, a young boy named Ethan. Ethan excelled in math early on, solving problems that left even his teachers in awe. However, he struggled with emotional outbursts, especially when facing challenges that did not come quickly. His parents enrolled him in a gifted program where he met other children who shared his passion for math. This provided him with intellectual stimulation and helped him develop better emotional regulation as he interacted with peers who understood his struggles.

Another example is Anna, a young artist whose advanced drawing skills were evident before she started kindergarten. Despite her artistic talents, she struggled to relate to her classmates, often feeling isolated and misunderstood. Her parents encouraged her to join an art club, where she met other young artists. This helped her build friendships based on shared interests, ease her social interactions, and boost her confidence.

The key is balance. While nurturing these children's intellectual abilities is essential, supporting their emotional and social development is equally vital. This means being patient and understanding, providing opportunities for them to engage with peers, and helping them navigate the complexities of their unique developmental path. Creating a supportive environment that acknowledges their strengths and challenges can help your child thrive in all aspects of life.

## 1.3 RECOGNIZING OVEREXCITABILITIES AND SENSITIVITIES

Ever wonder why your child seems to bounce off the walls after a long day at school or why a simple tag on a shirt turns into a full-blown meltdown? Welcome to the world of overexcitability, a concept that Polish psychologist Kazimierz Dabrowski brought to light. These heightened responses to stimuli aren't mere quirks;

they are core aspects of giftedness that can drive parents up the wall while also being incredibly fascinating.

Let us start with *psychomotor overexcitability*. If your child is constantly on the move, has endless energy, and seems incapable of sitting still, you have encountered this. These kids might be the ones who tap their feet incessantly during dinner or cannot resist the urge to run circles around the living room. Their restless energy needs an outlet, or it can quickly turn into frustration.

Then, there's *sensual overexcitability*, where children are sensitive to sounds, smells, textures, and other sensory inputs. Imagine a child who cannot stand the feeling of wool, recoils at certain smells, or is overwhelmed by loud noises. These sensitivities can make daily experiences, like getting dressed or going to a busy store, a minefield of potential triggers.

*Intellectual overexcitability* might be more familiar to you. These children show deep curiosity and an insatiable love for learning. They ask endless questions, often diving deeply into subjects beyond their age level. Their minds are constantly at work, pondering the mysteries of the universe or at least how the toaster works.

*Imaginational overexcitability* is where vivid imagination and daydreaming come into play. These kids might have imaginary friends, create elaborate stories, or lose themselves in fantasies. Their imaginative world is rich and detailed, sometimes making it hard to stay grounded.

*Emotional overexcitability* is probably the most challenging to manage. These children experience intense feelings and strong emotional reactions. A minor disappointment can lead to a torrent of tears, while a joyful moment can make them exuberant to exhaustion. Their emotional landscape is a rollercoaster that can be exhilarating yet draining.

Recognizing these overexcitabilities in your child can help you understand their behavior better. You might notice that they become easily overwhelmed by sensory input, like a noisy classroom or a crowded mall. Their deep emotional responses to stories or events can be touching and perplexing. Persistent questioning and deep thinking are hallmark behaviors of intellectual overexcitability.

Managing these overexcitabilities requires a thoughtful approach. Creating a sensory-friendly environment can help. This might mean noise-canceling headphones for a child sensitive to sound or soft, tag-free clothing for one who cannot stand certain textures. Teaching mindfulness and relaxation techniques can also be beneficial. Simple breathing exercises or guided meditation can help them manage their emotional intensity.

Another effective strategy is encouraging creative outlets for emotional expression. Art, music, and writing allow children to channel their intense emotions constructively. For instance, teenagers might find solace in painting or writing poetry to express their feelings, turning emotional turbulence into a source of creativity.

Jacob comes to mind here. He was a young boy who needed quiet time after school to decompress from sensory overload. His parents created a calm, peaceful space at home where he could retreat, helping him manage his sensory sensitivities. Emma is another example – a teenager who used art to express her intense emotions. Painting became her sanctuary, allowing her to process and healthily release her feelings.

Understanding and managing overexcitabilities can transform these kids' challenges into opportunities for growth and creativity. By recognizing these traits in your child and providing the proper support, you can help them navigate their heightened sensitivities and harness their unique strengths.

## 1.4 TWICE-EXCEPTIONAL CHILDREN: NAVIGATING DUAL NEEDS

Twice-exceptional children, or 2e children, are gifted yet also face learning disabilities. For instance, a young artist who creates breathtaking paintings but struggles with dyslexia or a budding mathematician who excels at complex calculations but has ADHD. These children are a bundle of contrasts, presenting remarkable strengths and significant challenges. Their dual needs often make navigating traditional educational settings a Herculean task, not just for them but also for their parents and educators.

The challenges faced by 2e children are multifaceted. Traditional school settings can be particularly tough. On one hand, their giftedness might need to be fully recognized or nurtured. On the other, their learning disabilities can overshadow their strengths, leading to misplaced expectations. Imagine a child who can solve advanced math problems but struggles to read the instructions. Teachers might mistake this for a lack of effort or interest rather than recognizing the dual nature of the child's abilities.

Misunderstandings by educators and peers add another layer of complexity. Peers might see a child who is brilliant in one area but struggles in another and fail to understand the incongruence. They might tease or ostracize, making social interactions fraught with difficulty. Educators, too, might need more training or resources to support these children adequately, leading to frustration on all sides.

Emotional and social challenges are shared. The mismatch between their intellectual capacities and their learning disabilities can lead to feelings of inadequacy, frustration, and low self-esteem. These children are often acutely aware of being different, making them feel isolated and misunderstood. It's a huge emotional toll on a child who knows they are capable of remarkable things but constantly bumps up against the limitations imposed by their disabilities.

So, how can parents support their 2e children effectively? Advocacy is key. Parents need to become strong advocates for appropriate accommodations in school. This might mean pushing for an Individualized Education Plan (IEP) that recognizes the child's giftedness and learning disabilities. Schools are required by law to provide accommodations, but it often takes persistent advocacy to meet these needs.

Specialized tutoring can also make a significant difference. Tutors who understand giftedness and learning disabilities can tailor their approach to meet the child's needs. Whether it is a math whiz with dyslexia or an artist with ADHD, specialized support can help these children thrive academically while also addressing their areas of difficulty.

Another vital strategy is to encourage strengths while supporting weaknesses. Celebrate these children's gifts and provide opportunities for them to shine, whether that is through advanced classes, art programs, or other enrichment activities. At the same time, offer support for their weaknesses. This might involve using assistive technology, providing extra time for tasks, or breaking down assignments into manageable chunks.

Consider the story of Alex, a student who excelled in art but struggled with dyslexia. With the proper support, Alex could participate in advanced art classes while receiving specialized tutoring for reading. This dual approach allowed Alex to thrive in both areas, boosting his academic performance, confidence, and self-esteem.

Another example is Mia, a child who excelled in math but had ADHD. With accommodations like extra time on tests and a quiet space for work, Mia could participate in advanced math classes without the usual distractions. Specialized tutoring helped her develop strategies to manage ADHD symptoms, making it easier to focus and succeed.

The key to supporting 2e children is recognizing their unique strengths and challenges. By advocating for appropriate accommodations, providing specialized support, and celebrating their gifts, parents can help these children navigate their dual needs and reach their full potential. The journey may be complex, but the path becomes more straightforward with understanding, patience, and strategies.

# EMOTIONAL AND PSYCHOLOGICAL INSIGHTS

## 2.1 UNDERSTANDING EMOTIONAL INTENSITY

Imagine entering your child's room and finding them in tears, clutching a crumpled drawing. You ask what is wrong, and they respond with a heartfelt lament about how their masterpiece did not turn out as they'd envisioned. In these moments, you realize your child does not just *feel* emotions, they experience them with the intensity of a supernova. This is the world of emotional intensity in gifted children, where feelings are vibrant and all-consuming, and your child's emotional barometer reads like a rollercoaster ride.

Emotional intensity in gifted children is more than just having big feelings; it is a complex trait that colors their entire world. These children embody emotions rather than just experience them. For instance, a triumph, like acing a spelling test, can send them into fits of joy that rival a cat with a new toy. Conversely, a setback, such as a less-than-perfect art project, can plunge them into deep despair. Emotional intensity also manifests in their incredible empathy. They do not merely sympathize with others' suffering; they feel it as if it were their own, often expressing profound concern for world events or a classmate's skinned knee.

Understanding the triggers and patterns of your child's emotional outbursts will assist you with navigating this intensity. Academic pressures, like looming deadlines or lofty expectations, can catalyze emotional upheaval. Social interactions can also stir the pot, with peer dynamics setting the stage for joy or heartache. Busy environments, with their cacophony of sounds and sights, can overwhelm their senses, leading to sensory overload that leaves these children frazzled. Recognizing these patterns helps you anticipate and mitigate potential meltdowns before they reach critical mass.

Managing this emotional intensity requires an arsenal of coping mechanisms. Teaching your child deep breathing techniques can offer them a lifeline in moments of distress. Also, encourage them to find solace in journaling or artistic expressions as this will provide an outlet for their cathartic and constructive feelings. Establishing a calming routine, a daily ritual of quiet time, or a bedtime story can anchor them in moments of emotional turbulence.

As a parent, your role is instrumental in supporting your child through their emotional highs and lows. Active listening is your superpower, allowing you to validate their feelings without judgment. Set consistent boundaries and provide structure, offering security in an unpredictable world—model emotional regulation through your behavior, showing them how to experience various emotions with grace and resilience.

*Reflection Exercise*

Consider keeping a journal to track your child's emotional triggers and responses. Note any patterns in their behavior and reflect on the strategies that have been most effective in helping them manage their emotions. Over time, you will build a personalized guide to your child's emotional landscape, empowering you to support them with empathy and understanding.

Try to remember that your child's heightened responses are not a burden but a gift. They hold the potential for immense joy, deep empathy, and a rich inner life that can fuel their passions and drive their achievements. Your understanding and support will help them navigate their emotional world with confidence and strength.

## 2.2 PERFECTIONISM AND ANXIETY: COPING STRATEGIES

Gifted children often carry the world's weight on their shoulders, and nowhere is this more evident than their struggle with perfectionism. This trait, while seemingly innocuous, can lead to a cascade of anxiety and self-doubt. Gifted children frequently set staggeringly high personal standards for themselves. They do not just want to do well, they want to excel in everything they attempt, from academics to hobbies, often setting the bar higher than is reasonable. This drive for perfection can create an intense fear of failure or making mistakes, as they equate errors with inadequacy. In their quest for flawlessness, they may constantly compare themselves to others, leading to feelings of inferiority when they perceive they have fallen short.

Parents need to recognize the symptoms of perfectionism and the anxiety it spawns. One telltale sign is procrastination. Yes, the same child who can explain string theory might delay starting a project because they fear it will not be perfect. They might avoid tasks they feel they cannot excel in, preferring not to try at all rather than risk imperfection. Excessive self-criticism is another red flag. These children focus on their flaws, often dismissing their achievements as not good enough. This relentless self-scrutiny can manifest physically, with headaches or stomachaches appearing as their anxiety takes a toll on their bodies.

To help your child manage this perfectionism, start by encouraging a growth mindset. Emphasizing that effort, not just the outcome, is what truly matters. Celebrate the whole learning process, including the mistakes made along the way. Help them set realistic and achievable goals, breaking tasks into manageable steps to prevent them from becoming overwhelmed. Praise their progress and resilience over perfection, reminding them that everyone makes mistakes and that these are opportunities to gain experience and grow.

Addressing the anxiety linked to perfectionism involves specific techniques. Mindfulness and meditation can be very helpful here as they teach your child to stay grounded in the present moment rather than spiraling into worry about what might go wrong. Consider creating a "worry time," a designated period where your child can voice their anxieties, freeing the rest of the day from their grip. If your child's anxiety becomes overwhelming, do not hesitate to seek professional help. A therapist can work wonders by providing your child with strategies to cope with their fears and develop healthier thought patterns.

### Reflection Section

Think about a recent situation where your child displayed signs of perfectionism. Reflect on how you respond and what you might do differently next time to support them in developing a healthier relationship with their achievements and failures. Please discuss this with your child, exploring their thoughts and feelings about perfection and mistakes.

In the dance between giftedness and perfectionism, the goal is not to extinguish their drive to excel but to channel it in ways that nourish growth and self-compassion. By understanding and addressing the root causes of their perfectionism and anxiety, you can help your child embrace their abilities without fear.

## 2.3 BUILDING EMOTIONAL RESILIENCE

Emotional resilience is the ability to bounce back from setbacks and develop a positive outlook on challenges that life inevitably brings. With their unique blend of elevated expectations and intense emotions, gifted children benefit immensely from learning how to dust themselves off and keep going when things do not go as planned.

However, building emotional resilience in a gifted child can be like trying to make a sandcastle at high tide. The waves of emotion come thick and fast and sometimes, just keeping the castle standing is a victory. However, bolstering resilience is essential for your child's long-term happiness and ability to cope with life's inevitable difficulties.

One way to build resilience is to encourage problem-solving and critical thinking. These academic and life skills can help your child navigate tricky emotional waters. When faced with a problem, whether a frustrating math puzzle or a friendship hiccup, encourage your child to think about different solutions and evaluate which might work best. This teaches them to manage challenges independently and builds their confidence in their ability to tackle whatever life throws their way.

Promoting self-care and healthy habits is another cornerstone of resilience. Teach your child the importance of taking breaks, getting enough sleep, and eating well. These habits provide a stable foundation upon which emotional resilience can grow. A child who is well-rested and well-nourished is better equipped to manage stress. Please encourage them to find activities that help them relax and recharge, whether it be reading, playing an instrument, or simply spending time in nature.

Creating a supportive family environment is like giving your child a warm, fluffy blanket to wrap themselves in during tough times. Open communication, where feelings are acknowledged and respected, is vital. Celebrate small victories and efforts with enthusiasm, even if it is something as simple as trying a new hobby or making a new friend. Providing constructive feedback helps them learn from experiences without feeling criticized. Encouraging independence and self-reliance teaches them that they have the strength to stand on their own two feet, even when the going gets tough.

Resilience-building activities can be fun and rewarding. Engaging in sports or team-based activities promotes physical health and teaches teamwork and perseverance. Participating in community service or volunteer work is a fantastic way for children to gain perspective and understand the value of giving back. Practicing gratitude journaling is a simple yet effective method to help children focus on the positives in their lives, promoting a more resilient mindset.

### Resilience Quiz

Create a short, fun quiz to identify areas where your child might already be showing resilience and where they could use more support. Questions might include: "How do you feel when you don't succeed at something right away?" or "What do you do to cheer yourself up when you're feeling down?"

In this unpredictable world, emotional resilience is a gift that keeps giving. By supporting your child in building these skills, you are helping them maneuver through the complexities of their giftedness and equipping them with the tools they need to thrive as well-rounded, emotionally intelligent individuals.

## 2.4 UNDERSTANDING AND ADDRESSING UNDERACHIEVEMENT

Underachievement in gifted children can be as perplexing as watching a cheetah choose to nap instead of taking a sprint. It is the gap between what they are capable of and what they accomplish. It's frustrating to have a child who has the potential to solve problems like a mini-Einstein but shows little interest in schoolwork or homework. This discrepancy often leaves parents scratching their heads and wondering where the motivation went. Gifted children might underachieve when their educational environment is not engaging enough or when personal factors like anxiety or depression sap their energy. Sometimes, the cause is simply a mismatch between the child's learning style and the school's teaching approach.

Identifying the roots of this underachievement requires a bit of detective work. Boredom is a common culprit. A curriculum that does not challenge or stimulate can lead to disengagement, making school feel more like a chore than an opportunity. Emotional issues like anxiety or depression can also act like invisible weights that hold a child back from reaching their potential. Additionally, learning disabilities or other twice-exceptionalities can complicate the picture, creating barriers the child might not know how to overcome. Understanding these underlying causes will help you to formulate a plan to address them.

How can you help your child overcome this underachievement and shine brightly? First, provide opportunities for enrichment and advanced learning. Supplement their schoolwork with activities that pique their interest, like science camps, art classes, or coding workshops. These activities can reignite their passion for learning, proving that education can be engaging and fun. Setting specific, achievable goals and tracking progress can also make a difference. Break tasks into smaller steps and celebrate each milestone. This approach makes goals more attainable and provides a sense of accomplishment with every step forward.

Encourage your child to tackle passion projects or areas of interest. Whether it is building robots, drafting stories, or exploring astronomy, these projects can provide a much-needed outlet for their talents and creativity. They also allow your child to take ownership of their learning, nurturing a sense of autonomy and motivation. Let them explore topics that genuinely excite them without the pressure of grades or external expectations.

Consider the story of Daniel, a bright student who had become disengaged with the traditional school setting. His parents noticed his lack of enthusiasm for schoolwork and decided to connect him with a mentorship program focused on engineering, the subject that had once captivated him. Through hands-on projects and one-on-one guidance, Daniel found his spark again, reigniting his love for learning and bolstering his academic performance.

Then there's Sophia, who struggled in a mainstream classroom that did not cater to her unique learning style. Her parents enrolled her in a specialized education setting designed for gifted students. Here, the curriculum was tailored to her needs and provided the right balance of challenge and support. Sophia thrived in this environment, both academically, socially, and emotionally.

While underachievement can be frustrating, it is not a dead end. With the proper support and strategies, your child can break free from the confines of underachievement and soar to new heights. By understanding their unique needs and providing opportunities that align with their interests, you are paving the way for them to reach their full potential. As you move forward, remember that each child is a unique puzzle. Sometimes, the pieces do not fit perfectly at first, but with patience and creativity, they eventually come together.

As we close this chapter, we see that giftedness's emotional and psychological facets are as varied as they are profound. Understanding these elements helps unlock the potential within each gifted child. With this foundation laid, we now focus on practical strategies for everyday life, where the theories meet reality and where you can make an immediate difference.

# PRACTICAL STRATEGIES FOR DAILY LIFE

## 3.1 TEACHING AND PRACTICING EFFECTIVE COMMUNICATION

Picture this scenario: you are trying to cook dinner, the phone is ringing, and your gifted child is in front of you, passionately debating the pros and cons of colonizing Mars. They are not just talking; they are presenting a full-fledged argument, complete with data, while you are trying to remember if you add salt to the pasta. In these moments, the importance of effective communication with your child becomes glaringly apparent. They think faster than a supercomputer and keeping up with their thoughts requires more than just a nod and a smile!

Maintaining open lines of communication with your gifted child is more than beneficial, it is necessary. These children often have deep thoughts and unique perspectives that need to be heard and understood. It starts with active listening, which means paying attention, not just waiting for your speech. Show empathy and understanding by nodding, making eye contact, and using encouraging phrases like, "Tell me more about that." Encourage them to freely express their thoughts and feelings, thereby creating a safe sharing environment. Avoid dismissive language or invalidating their experiences, as this can shut down communication faster than a power outage.

Using specific techniques can be incredibly helpful in promoting productive and respectful conversations. One such technique is the use of "I" statements. This involves expressing your feelings without placing blame, such as saying, "I feel worried when you don't tell me how you're feeling," instead of, "You never tell me anything!" This method can reduce defensiveness and open the door to honest dialogue.

Reflective listening is another effective instrument. This involves repeating what your child has said to ensure you understand and show them that you are truly listening. It might feel awkward initially, like you are mimicking them, but it works. Setting aside dedicated time for daily check-ins or family meetings can also help. These moments provide a structured opportunity for everyone to share their thoughts and feelings in a safe space.

Difficult conversations are inevitable, but they do not have to be daunting. Staying calm and composed during emotional outbursts is critical. Your child might be a whirlwind of emotions, but your steady presence can be the eye of the storm. Use positive reinforcement to acknowledge their bravery in sharing difficult emotions. A simple "I'm proud of you for telling me how you feel" can be impactful. Establishing clear boundaries and expectations provides a framework for these conversations, helping reduce anxiety and misunderstandings.

Encouraging self-advocacy in your child is a gift that keeps on giving. Teach them to speak up for their needs by role-playing scenarios that might arise, both at home and in school. This can be as simple as practicing asking a teacher for help or respectfully expressing disagreement. Encourage them to articulate their needs and preferences clearly. This boosts their confidence and prepares them for real-world interactions where they might need to stand up for themselves.

### Reflection Activity: Communication Journal

Try keeping a communication journal with your child. After each meaningful conversation, jot down what was discussed, how it was managed, and what you both learned from it. Reflect on what went well and what could be improved. This practice can enhance your communication skills and deepen your understanding of each other.

In the storm of daily life with a gifted child, effective communication is the anchor that keeps the ship steady. By promoting open dialogue, understanding, and respect, you are connecting with your child and building a relationship that will support them through the complexities of their giftedness.

## 3.2 BEHAVIOR MANAGEMENT: POSITIVE REINFORCEMENT AND DISCIPLINE

Think of your gifted child as a young explorer, navigating the world with a sense of wonder and an occasional disregard for parental warnings about the hot stove. Behavior management is the sturdy compass guiding them through this journey.

For gifted children, typical behavioral strategies can fall short. They require a nuanced approach that considers their intense curiosity and emotional sensitivity. This approach's heart lies in the distinction between positive reinforcement and punishment. Positive reinforcement involves rewarding desired behaviors to encourage repetition, whereas punishment seeks to curb undesirable actions through negative consequences. While punishment may yield immediate compliance, positive reinforcement supports long-term growth and a more harmonious relationship.

Implementing positive reinforcement in daily life can transform how your child interacts with the world. Start by rewarding effort and progress, not just outcomes. This simple shift encourages a growth mindset, teaching them that persistence, rather than perfection, is what matters. You might introduce a reward system using stickers, points, or privileges. For instance, when your child completes homework without a fuss, they earn a sticker. Collect enough stickers, and they might choose the family movie for the weekend. Verbal praise is equally powerful. Specific praise like, "I noticed how you shared your toys with your brother," reinforces positive behavior and builds self-esteem.

Effective discipline techniques are critical for setting boundaries and maintaining order. Begin by setting clear and consistent rules. These should be reasonable and age appropriate as a framework for acceptable behavior. When these rules get broken, they implement natural consequences. For example, if your child refuses to wear a coat, let them experience the cold briefly, teaching them the importance of listening. Time-outs can help cool down emotional outbursts, providing a moment for reflection. Also, teaching problem-solving and conflict-resolution skills equips your child to manage disputes independently. Encourage them to articulate their feelings and brainstorm solutions, guiding them toward peaceful resolutions.

Addressing specific behavioral issues in gifted children requires understanding and immense patience. For instance, managing defiance and non-compliance can be challenging. Gifted children often question rules, seeking to understand their purpose. Engage them in discussions about the reasoning behind regulations, thereby building a sense of autonomy and respect. Address impulsivity and hyperactivity by providing structured outlets for their energy. Activities like sports or creative projects can channel their enthusiasm productively.

Sibling rivalry and jealousy often rear their ugly heads in households with gifted children. The intensity of their emotions can amplify these feelings, leading to dramatic battles over who gets the last cookie. Encourage communication and empathy among siblings. Teach them to express their feelings constructively and acknowledge one another's achievements. Set aside time with each child to reinforce their unique strengths and nurture their self-worth.

### Visual Element: Positive Reinforcement Chart

You could try creating a positive reinforcement chart. On it, list desired behaviors along with corresponding rewards. Use stickers or checkmarks to track progress. This visual tool reinforces the connection between actions and rewards and should motivate your child to continue making positive choices.

In the unpredictable world of parenting gifted children, behavior management is not about control. It is about understanding their unique needs and guiding them toward self-discipline and emotional maturity. By embracing positive reinforcement and consistent discipline, you give them the resources to walk through the world with confidence and respect.

## 3.3 CREATING A STIMULATING HOME ENVIRONMENT

Your home is a playground for your child's mind, where curiosity and exploration are encouraged. A stimulating home environment nourishes gifted children's intellectual and emotional growth. These kids have an inbuilt eagerness to learn. Their innate desire to explore and discover will stay strong in the right environment. To nurture it, allow them to ask questions, make discoveries, and learn independently. This does not mean turning your living room into a science lab (though that could be fun) but instead cultivating an atmosphere where learning feels as natural as breathing.

Try to design adequate learning spaces at home. Perhaps set up a quiet study area, free from the distractions of TV noise and sibling squabbles. It will be a corner that invites focus and contemplation, with comfortable seating and proper lighting to keep the eyes relaxed and the mind alert. Provide access to various books, educational games, and resources. Think of it as a buffet for the brain where you offer your child a variety of intellectual dishes to sample and savor. Whether it's a stack of diverse books or a collection of intriguing puzzles, having these resources within arm's reach can ignite a spark of curiosity and keep it burning bright.

Incorporating enrichment activities into daily routines doesn't take much effort. You just need to remember to make everyday moments into learning opportunities. For instance, searing a piece of meat over the fire or baking a loaf of bread can become hands-on science experiments or sewing and mending can become art projects. These everyday tasks provide tactile experiences that engage the senses and stimulate the mind. Imagine your child's delight as they create a volcano out of baking soda and vinegar in the kitchen sink that erupts! Alternatively, watch as they craft a masterpiece using imagination and a few simple art supplies. Family game nights with educational board games can turn a regular evening into a fun-filled learning session. These games entertain and teach valuable skills like strategy and cooperation. Virtual museum tours or educational documentaries can transport your child to distant lands and ancient times, all from the comfort of your living room.

Balancing structure and flexibility in your child's routine is essential for instilling discipline and creativity. Creating a daily schedule with designated learning and play time provides structure, helping your child develop a sense of routine and responsibility. However, it is equally important to allow room for flexibility, accommodating spontaneous activities and interests that might arise. This balance ensures that your child can explore self-directed projects and hobbies. One day, they may decide to build a model of the solar system, and another they'll draft a short story about a time-traveling detective. Encouraging these pursuits can lead to unexpected discoveries and new passions.

### Interactive Element: Home Environment Self-Assessment

Conduct a home environment assessment with your child. Walk through your home together and identify areas that can be enhanced to promote learning and creativity. Discuss what resources or changes might inspire them to explore their interests further. This activity will empower your child and strengthen your connection as you collaborate on shaping their learning environment.

Your home is more than just a place to eat and sleep; it is a dynamic space where your child's mind can flourish. By creating an environment that encourages curiosity and exploration, you'll give them the foundation to grow into confident, independent thinkers.

## 3.4 TIME MANAGEMENT FOR BUSY FAMILIES

Picture this: you are juggling a dozen tasks, and your gifted child announces that they've signed up for the school robotics competition, which coincides with piano lessons and your long-anticipated dentist appointment. Welcome to the circus act of balancing a busy family schedule. For families with gifted children, time management can feel like trying to solve a Rubik's cube with one hand tied behind your back. Balancing school, extracurricular activities and family time is an intricate dance that requires precision and flexibility. The challenge is compounded by parental work commitments, which often demand your attention when your child needs help with their science project, or you are due at a parent-teacher meeting.

Effective time management techniques are your best allies if you want to tame the chaos. Calendars and planners are lifelines for busy families. They help you schedule activities and deadlines, ensuring nothing slips through the cracks. Whether digital or old-school paper, visually representing your family's commitments can clarify and reduce stress. They allow you to prioritize tasks and set realistic goals. Once everything is "on paper," you'll be able to see what really matters and let go of the less critical tasks. Implementing routines for morning and bedtime can streamline your daily flow, ensuring everyone knows what to expect and minimizing last-minute scrambles for lost shoes or forgotten lunchboxes.

Involving your child in time management makes the whole process even more interesting. With their intense curiosity and myriad interests, gifted children thrive when given autonomy over their schedules. Encourage the use of age-appropriate planners or apps to help them track their activities. This instills a sense of responsibility and teaches valuable organizational skills. Guide them in setting and managing their goals. Whether completing a book by the end of the week or practicing the violin for thirty minutes daily, having personal objectives can be incredibly motivating. Allow them to help create the family schedule, giving them a voice in time allocation. This collaborative approach can lead to surprising insights and innovative solutions.

Balancing multiple priorities without feeling overwhelmed is no small feat. It starts with learning to say *no* to non-essential activities. As tempting as filling every slot with enrichment opportunities might be, sometimes the best choice is to let your child have a little downtime to just "be." Delegate tasks among family members to lighten the load. Chores become less daunting when shared, and children enjoy taking on responsibilities when they feel valued. Scheduling regular downtime for the whole is important too. Whether it is an evening of board games or a quiet afternoon at the park, these moments of relaxation and connection recharge everyone's batteries.

In the grand scheme of things, time management involves more than just fitting everything into a tightly packed schedule. It also includes making space for what truly matters, ensuring that amidst the hustle and bustle, there's room for laughter, love, and learning. As you find solutions to these practical challenges, remember that your efforts are going toward creating a life that aligns with your family's values and aspirations.

Next, we'll move on to the next chapter which is about exploring educational pathways and advocacy and how to navigate the school system to support your gifted child best.

# EDUCATIONAL PATHWAYS AND ADVOCACY

## 4.1 YOUR INVOLVEMENT MAKES AN ENORMOUS DIFFERENCE

Many parents of gifted children face the challenge of navigating traditional schooling to ensure their child receives an education that aligns with their advanced abilities and curiosity. As discussions around curriculum changes occur at PTA meetings, parents often experience a mix of anticipation and concern, as these meetings can feel competitive, with differing views on the best educational options for their children.

Traditional schooling, with its standardized curriculum, classroom-based learning, and state-mandated assessments, is the default educational path for many children. In this environment, every child is expected to learn the same material at the same pace, much like a one-size-fits-all sweater that fits nobody quite right. For some, this predictability offers comfort. The structured learning environment provides a reliable framework many parents appreciate, with set schedules and expectations. Your child will find themselves in a bustling classroom where peer socialization occurs daily. This interaction is vital, as it helps develop people skills and friendships that can last a lifetime. Moreover, traditional schools often offer an array of extracurricular activities, from chess clubs to drama groups, allowing your child to explore interests beyond academics.

However, for gifted children, traditional schooling can sometimes feel like trying to run a marathon in flip-flops. One of the main drawbacks is the lack of individualized attention. Despite their best intentions, teachers often must juggle large class sizes and diverse needs, making it challenging to provide personalized support to each student. This can lead to inadequate acceleration opportunities, where your child might find themselves yawning through lessons they have already mastered. The risk of boredom and underachievement looms, as the standard curriculum may not challenge gifted children sufficiently. This can result in disengagement and a lack of enthusiasm for learning, which is the last thing any parent wants for their child.

Fear not, for there are strategies you can employ to maximize the benefits of traditional schooling for your gifted child. For a start, it's possible to advocate for differentiated instruction. This approach tailors teaching methods to accommodate various learning styles and paces, ensuring your child remains engaged and challenged. Next, you must try to build a solid relationship with teachers and school administrators. Regular communication and collaboration can open doors to opportunities that would otherwise remain closed.

Supplementing school learning with enrichment activities can also work wonders. Introducing your child to a world of knowledge beyond the classroom through visits to museums, science camps, or online courses. These experiences can reignite their passion for learning and provide the intellectual stimulation they crave.

As a parent, your role is invaluable. By actively participating in your child's education, you can ensure their unique needs are met and their brilliance is nurtured.

*Reflection Section: Maximizing Traditional Schooling*

Take a moment to reflect on your child's current schooling experience. Are there areas where they seem disengaged or unchallenged? If so, schedule a meeting with their teacher to discuss potential strategies for differentiation or enrichment. Explore local resources or online platforms that offer advanced learning opportunities. Your involvement can make a world of difference in their educational journey.

## 4.2 HOMESCHOOLING: TAILORING EDUCATION TO FIT YOUR CHILD

Picture this: It is a Tuesday morning, and instead of the usual rush to catch the school bus, you and your child are sitting at the kitchen table, sipping hot chocolate and performing a science experiment about volcanos. Homeschooling offers unique flexibility that allows you to create an educational experience tailored to your child's abilities and interests. Unlike traditional schooling, homeschooling enables you to design a personalized curriculum that can adapt to your child's pace and passions. This flexibility means you can spend an entire week exploring ancient Egypt's wonders, if that captures your child's imagination, without worrying about fitting into a rigid schedule.

For gifted children, homeschooling can be a breath of fresh air. It allows you to customize the pace and content of lessons to match your child's unique abilities. If your child breezes through math problems faster than you can say, "Pythagorean theorem," you can adjust the curriculum to keep them challenged and engaged. This flexibility also extends to creating a stress-free learning environment. Traditional classrooms can sometimes feel like pressure cookers, but in the comfort of your home, you can make a space where learning feels more like an adventure and less like a chore. Integrating your child's interests and passions into the curriculum is another significant advantage. Whether they are fascinated by dinosaurs, space exploration, or medieval history, you can weave these interests into their lessons, making education a truly personalized experience.

However, homeschooling is not all sunshine and rainbows. It requires a considerable commitment of time and resources from parents. You become a full-time educator, which can be challenging to balance with other responsibilities. There is also the potential for social isolation, as homeschooled children may have fewer daily opportunities to interact with peers than those in traditional schools. This means parents must proactively seek social opportunities for their children, whether through playgroups, sports teams, or community activities. As the primary educator, you must stay updated on the best educational practices, which can feel daunting. This requires research, attending workshops, or joining online communities to ensure you provide your child with the best possible education.

Fortunately, there are plenty of resources and support systems available for homeschooling families. Homeschooling co-ops and networks can provide a sense of community, offering opportunities for group learning and social interaction. These networks often organize field trips, classes, and events, allowing your child to meet and learn with other homeschooled children. Online curriculum providers and educational platforms are also invaluable, offering a wealth of resources and materials that can supplement your teaching. These tools can enhance your child's learning experience and provide additional support, from interactive math programs to virtual science labs. Local and national homeschooling organizations can also be a reliable source of information and encouragement. They often offer workshops, conferences, and online forums where you can connect with other homeschooling parents and share experiences, challenges, and triumphs.

While homeschooling presents many challenges, it can also offer an enriching educational experience tailored to your child's unique needs. This approach requires dedication and creativity, but the rewards can be significant. Providing a learning environment that nurtures your child's interests, accommodates their pace, and promotes growth can lead to incredible outcomes.

## 4.3 SPECIALIZED PROGRAMS AND SCHOOLS

Specialized programs and schools for gifted children offer unique educational environments tailored to their advanced abilities. These institutions include magnet schools that focus on specific subjects, providing a curriculum that emphasizes science, technology, engineering, and math (STEM). Additionally, Gifted and Talented Education (GATE) programs challenge students beyond the standard curriculum, promoting intellectual growth through differentiated instruction and enrichment activities. Private schools with advanced curricula also cater to gifted learners, often featuring smaller class sizes and resources designed to provide a more personalized learning experience.

Specialized education caters to the unique needs of gifted children in a way that traditional settings may not. Access to advanced coursework and resources allows these students to engage with material that matches their intellectual abilities, preventing the boredom that often accompanies unchallenging mainstream classes. Opportunities for intellectual peer interactions are abundant, as students are surrounded by like-minded individuals who share their curiosity and zeal for learning. This environment nurtures academic excellence and promotes a sense of belonging and mutual understanding. Specialized teaching methods and materials cater to the diverse learning styles of gifted students, ensuring that each child can thrive in a way that suits them best. Teachers in these settings are often trained to recognize and nurture the potential of gifted students, offering support and guidance that encourages academic and personal development.

Finding the right fit for your child in specialized education requires thorough research and consideration. Start by exploring different programs and their educational philosophies to determine which aligns best with your child's needs and interests and your family's culture. Visit schools, meet with administrators and teachers, and observe classes if possible. These visits provide valuable insights into the school's environment and approach to education. Notice how the school addresses the specific needs of gifted students and whether they offer the necessary resources and support. Assess the school's ability to provide opportunities for your child to grow academically and socially, ensuring that it aligns with your expectations and goals. A school that instills a love for learning and nurtures your child's potential is worth its weight in gold.

Real-life success stories paint a vivid picture of the impact specialized programs can have on gifted children. Take, for instance, the story of Alex, a student who found his stride in a science-focused magnet school. Here, Alex could explore his passion for biology, participating in hands-on experiments and research projects that ignited his curiosity. The school's emphasis on experiential learning and peer collaboration allowed Alex to thrive academically and socially.

Similarly, Sarah's experience in a private school for gifted learners transformed her educational journey. With access to specialized resources and individualized support, Sarah excelled in mathematics, a subject she had once found daunting in a traditional setting. The school's nurturing environment and focus on holistic development helped Sarah build confidence and resilience, empowering her to pursue her dreams.

These testimonials highlight the transformative power of specialized education, proving that the possibilities are endless when gifted children are placed in an environment that recognizes and nurtures their abilities.

## 4.4 WRITING AND IMPLEMENTING A GIFTED IEP

Navigating the education system for gifted children can feel like trying to find your way through a labyrinth without a map. However, there is a resource that can help guide you: the Gifted Individualized Education Plan, or IEP. This is a customized plan designed to cater to the unique needs of your gifted child. Think of it as a personalized blueprint for their educational journey. A Gifted IEP aims to set personalized educational goals, provide specific accommodations and modifications, and ensure regular progress monitoring. You'll be building a framework that supports your child's growth and learning in a way that makes sense for them.

Creating an effective IEP involves a few main steps, starting with requesting an IEP meeting with the school. This is your chance to sit down with educators and specialists to discuss your child's needs and how best to meet them. Collaboration is important here. You aren't a passive participant but a vital part of the team working to create a plan that reflects your child's strengths and challenges. During these meetings, it is important to set measurable and achievable goals. Identify what success looks like for your child and establish clear markers for their progress. These goals should be specific enough to provide direction but flexible enough to adapt as your child grows and changes.

Advocating for your child's needs during IEP meetings can sometimes feel intense but if you go in prepared, it won't feel as daunting. Start by gathering documentation and evidence of your child's giftedness. This could include test scores, teacher observations, or work examples highlighting their abilities. Communicate clearly and assertively, ensuring your voice is heard and your child's needs are understood. Ensuring the IEP includes appropriate accommodations and enrichment opportunities tailored to your child's unique talents is essential. This might mean advanced coursework, access to specialized resources, or creative and intellectual exploration opportunities.

Once the IEP is in place, monitoring and revising it ensures its success. Schedule regular review meetings with the school to discuss how the plan works and where adjustments might be needed. It's a living document that evolves with your child, growing and adapting as they do. Adjust goals and accommodations as needed, ensuring the IEP serves your child's best interests. Celebrate progress and address challenges openly, promoting a positive and proactive approach to your child's education.

In crafting a Gifted IEP, you create a document and build a partnership with educators and specialists to support your child's learning journey. You'll ensure they have the tools and opportunities to explore their potential fully. As we explore educational pathways, we will continue to look at strategies that empower you to advocate for and support your gifted child's unique needs.

# SOCIAL SKILLS AND PEER RELATIONSHIPS

## 5.1 FINDING AND KEEPING FRIENDS

You know your child's gifted when you overhear them explaining Plato's Allegory of the Cave to their teddy bears. As charming as it is to watch them enlighten the stuffed masses, it is a reminder that finding real-life peers who can engage with their intellectual musings is crucial. Gifted children often crave friendships beyond playing tag or discussing the latest superhero movie. They yearn for intellectual stimulation, that electric buzz of deep, meaningful conversations that make them feel understood and valued. It is not just about finding someone who can keep up with their mental gymnastics; it is about finding a friend who shares their quirky interests and passions.

The need for like-minded peers stems from the desire for connection and understanding. When your child finds someone who shares their enthusiasm for coding or astronomy, it is like discovering an oasis in the social desert. Engaging in conversations about shared interests provides them with a sense of belonging and validation, which is often missing in interactions with age-mates who might not understand their jokes about quantum physics or their fascination with ancient history. This shared intellectual playground offers a space where gifted children can explore, learn, and challenge one another, fueling their passion for discovery.

Helping your child find these kindred spirits will require detective work on your part. One effective strategy is enrolling them in specialized camps or workshops. These programs often attract children with similar interests and abilities, providing a fertile ground for friendships to blossom. Whether it is a coding camp that delves into the intricacies of algorithms or a creative writing workshop that encourages imaginative storytelling, these settings offer a natural environment for your child to connect with peers who "get it." Another approach is joining clubs or organizations focused on robotics, chess, or writing. These clubs will nurture your child's talents and introduce them to a community of like-minded individuals who share their enthusiasm and curiosity.

Creating social opportunities for your child to interact with potential friends is another piece of the puzzle. Hosting themed playdates or study groups can be a fantastic way to encourage social interactions in a comfortable setting. For instance, you could do a science-themed playdate where kids experiment with baking soda and vinegar volcanoes or a book club meeting where young readers discuss their favorite fantasy novels.

Participating in online communities or forums for gifted children can also provide a platform for connecting with peers who share similar interests, especially if geographical distance is a barrier.

Attending local events like science fairs or art exhibitions offers another avenue for meeting like-minded individuals, sparking conversations, and forming connections.

Supporting your child in developing and maintaining friendships is a big part of the process. Teaching social skills such as active listening and empathy can help them traverse the complexities of relationships. Do encourage them to communicate regularly with their friends through phone calls, video chats, or good old-fashioned letter writing. Modeling healthy friendships through your relationships is another influential teaching aid. Let your child see how you maintain connections, resolve conflicts, and support your friends as this will provide them with a roadmap for their interactions.

**Interactive Element: Friendship Journal**

Encourage your child to keep a friendship journal. In it, they can jot down thoughts about their interactions with peers, reflect on what they enjoy about their friendships, and brainstorm ways to strengthen these connections. This exercise increases self-awareness and helps them develop the skills to nurture and sustain meaningful relationships.

As you navigate the social landscape with your child, remember that finding like-minded peers requires patience, creativity, and a dash of humor. Your support and encouragement can make all the difference, helping your child build connections that enrich their lives and fuel their passions for years.

## 5.2 DEALING WITH BULLYING AND SOCIAL ISOLATION

When a child experiences sudden changes in behavior, such as becoming withdrawn when they're usually chatty and bubbly or losing interest in favorite activities, it may indicate they are facing bullying. Parents should be aware of these signs, as reluctance to go to school and unexplained physical injuries or damaged belongings can be red flags. Recognizing these indicators is essential for identifying when a child may need support in addressing bullying and its effects.

Once you suspect bullying, acting is paramount. Start by communicating with school officials and teachers. They are your allies in this fight and can provide insights into what might be happening during school hours. Documenting incidents and maintaining records is essential. Write down dates, times, and details of any bullying episodes your child reports. This information helps you keep track and serves as evidence if you need to escalate the issue. Encourage your child to speak up and assert themselves. While it is not easy, empowering them to voice their concerns can be a powerful antidote to the helplessness that often accompanies bullying.

Building resilience against bullying can transform your child from a target into a fortress. Teaching them problem-solving and conflict-resolution skills equips them with tools to traverse challenging social situations. Enrolling your child in self-defense classes can boost confidence and provide practical self-protection skills. However, don't underestimate the power of a supportive home environment. Create a haven where your child feels safe and heard. Let them vent, cry, or even rage. Your home should be a sanctuary where they can recharge their emotional batteries.

Preventing social isolation is another challenge that requires a proactive approach. Encourage your child to get involved in extracurricular activities. Whether joining a dance class, signing up for art lessons, or participating in a local sports team, these activities offer a chance to meet new people and form positive connections. Facilitate opportunities for social interactions outside of school. Arrange playdates, organize group outings, or plan family get-togethers. These interactions allow your child to practice social skills in a low-pressure environment. Promoting self-esteem and confidence through positive reinforcement is also important. Celebrate their achievements, no matter how small, and remind them of their strengths and capabilities. Confidence can be the best shield against bullying and isolation.

### Reflection Activity: Confidence Journal

Encourage your child to keep a *Confidence Journal*. Prompt them to write about their daily achievements and things they like about themselves. This practice can help reinforce positive self-perception and build resilience against negative experiences.

As you pilot your child through the complexities of bullying and social isolation, remember that your role is not just that of a protector but also an encourager and coach. Your support can make all the difference, helping your child emerge stronger and more confident from these challenges.

## 5.3 ENCOURAGING TEAMWORK AND COLLABORATION

Sometimes your child, who can recite the periodic table backward, may struggle with simple things like sharing their toys with others. While their intellectual abilities may be impressive, it's also important for them to develop teamwork and collaboration skills. Gifted children often excel independently but learning to share ideas and compromise is essential for their social development. In a world where most achievements are a team effort, understanding how to work with others is a skill they will use throughout life. By collaborating, they learn to appreciate diverse perspectives, which can enhance their creativity and problem-solving abilities. Additionally, developing leadership and followership skills in group settings teaches them to guide others while respecting distinct roles and contributions.

To promote teamwork and collaboration, try engaging your child in group projects at school or extracurricular clubs. These environments provide a structured setting where children can practice working with others and learn the dynamics of team interactions. Team sports or cooperative games are also great avenues for teaching collaboration. Through these activities, children learn to rely on teammates, communicate effectively, and celebrate collective successes. Community service projects that require group effort can further reinforce these skills. Working toward a common goal, such as organizing a food drive or participating in a neighborhood clean-up, teaches children the value of contributing to a more significant cause and instills a sense of responsibility.

Teaching practical collaboration skills involves more than just placing children in group settings. Assigning roles and responsibilities in these groups can help children understand and appreciate the importance of each team member's contribution. Encourage open communication and active listening by reminding your child to hear others out and consider their viewpoints. Practicing problem-solving as a team builds resilience and adaptability as children learn to take on challenges together. These experiences enhance their ability to work in a team and boost their confidence in their ability to contribute meaningfully.

As a parent, you can promote a collaborative mindset at home by engaging in activities that require teamwork. Working together on household chores and projects, like gardening or cooking, can be fun and is a great way to practice collaboration. Promote family discussions and decision-making, encouraging each member to voice their opinions and contribute. This approach models effective teamwork and demonstrates that everyone's input is valued.

Whether completing a family puzzle or decorating a room together, celebrating team achievements and successes reinforces the joy of working together and builds a sense of unity.

### Interactive Element: Family Collaboration Challenge

What about introducing a "Family Collaboration Challenge" at home? Choose a project that requires teamwork, such as building a birdhouse or planning a family outing. Assign roles and responsibilities to each family member, encouraging everyone to contribute ideas and solutions. Reflect on the process afterward, discussing what worked well and could be improved. This activity strengthens family bonds and provides a practical opportunity to practice teamwork and collaboration.

Collaboration is the thread that binds us together in the grand tapestry of life. By nurturing your child's ability to work with others, you equip them with skills that will serve them well in any endeavor. Whether debating the merits of a group project or leading a community initiative, their ability to collaborate will open doors to new opportunities and enrich their experiences.

## 5.4 TEACHING EMPATHY AND EMOTIONAL INTELLIGENCE

It's so rewarding as parents when our kids learn the art of socializing. It can also be nerve-wracking, especially when emotions run high! Empathy and emotional intelligence are your child's secret weapons to build solid relationships and sail through social interactions with grace. These skills are the foundation for mutual understanding and sensitivity, allowing your child to connect deeply with others. When your child understands how their words and actions affect those around them, they can better handle friendships, collaborations, and even the occasional playground drama. They need to learn when to listen or speak and to tune into others' emotional frequency and respond with kindness and awareness.

Teaching empathy takes time and patience. One effective technique is to encourage perspective-taking. Helping your child see situations from others' viewpoints enables them to develop a deeper understanding of different feelings and experiences. Open discussions about emotions and feelings create a safe space to express themselves and understand others. This practice can be as simple as asking, "How do you think your friend felt when you shared your toy?" or "How would you feel if someone did that to you?" Books and movies are lovely resources here, offering stories that explore diverse experiences and emotions. They can spark conversations and provide examples of empathy in action, helping your child learn from the characters' triumphs and mistakes.

Developing emotional intelligence in your child involves nurturing several vital skills. Begin with teaching self-awareness, helping them recognize their own emotions and understanding how these feelings influence their thoughts and actions. This can be done by naming emotions when they arise, like saying, "I see you're feeling frustrated because of the game." Practicing self-regulation and managing emotional responses is the next step. Techniques like deep breathing or counting to ten before reacting can be beneficial. These strategies give your child ways to manage their emotions without being overwhelmed. Enhancing social skills through role-playing and social stories allows them to practice responses to different scenarios, preparing them for real-life interactions. These exercises can be fun and engaging, providing a safe space to explore various emotional reactions and outcomes. An example is to pretend to phone someone who is sick. What would they say? How would they end the conversation?

To cultivate empathy and emotional intelligence, several activities can engage your child meaningfully. Participating in volunteer work or community service offers a firsthand perspective on the challenges others face, encouraging compassion and empathy. Mindfulness and reflective practices can enhance self-awareness and emotional regulation, teaching your child to pause and reflect before reacting. Playing cooperative games that require understanding and teamwork can reinforce these skills in a playful setting, promoting empathy, camaraderie, and cooperation.

### Interactive Element: Empathy Role-Play

Try an empathy role-play exercise with your child. Create a few scenarios that involve different emotions and social situations. Take turns acting them out, and afterward, discuss how each person might feel and why. This activity can deepen your child's understanding of empathy and provide practical experience in practicing it.

Empathy and emotional intelligence greatly enhance human interaction. By building these skills in your child, you prepare them for social success and help them build a world where understanding and kindness are the norm. These abilities will serve them well as they grow, opening doors to meaningful connections and enriching their lives in ways that pure intellect cannot. With these tools, your child will be able to face the world confidently, navigating the complexities of human relationships with the wisdom of a seasoned diplomat and the heart of a compassionate friend.

# CULTIVATING CREATIVITY AND CRITICAL THINKING

## 6.1 UNLOCKING CREATIVE POTENTIAL: THE POWER OF DIVERGENT THINKING IN GIFTED CHILDREN

Imagine watching your gifted child as they sit, surrounded by Legos, and you realize they are not just building a house, they are constructing a futuristic city complete with hovercrafts and solar panels. This is the essence of divergent thinking, a skill that allows children to break free from conventional thought patterns and explore a world where multiple solutions exist for a single problem. Divergent thinking doesn't just find a way to get from point A to point B; it maps out the entire alphabet! It encourages flexibility and originality in thinking, which are necessary for problem-solving. Gifted children often thrive in environments that challenge them to think creatively so cultivating this ability is like giving them a key to unlocking their full creative potential.

Developing divergent thinking skills in your child is a fun and rewarding journey. One effective technique is brainstorming sessions, focusing on quantity over quality. During such sessions, encourage your child to generate as many ideas as possible without worrying whether they are practical or feasible. This approach helps them learn that every idea has value and that the best solutions often come from a pool of possibilities. After the initial flood of ideas, guide them to refine and develop the most promising ones. Another valuable "game" is mind mapping, which involves visualizing connections between different concepts. This exercise can help your child see the bigger picture and understand how ideas are interrelated. By mapping out their thoughts, they can explore new avenues and make connections that might not be immediately obvious.

Engaging in "what if" scenarios is another way to stretch your child's imagination and encourage divergent thinking. Pose hypothetical situations and challenge them to explore various outcomes. Ask questions like, "What if animals could talk?" or "What if we lived on Mars?" These scenarios can spark creativity and lead to fascinating discussions that stretch the boundaries of conventional thinking. By encouraging your child to embrace curiosity and wonder, you'll nurture a mindset that welcomes exploration and innovation.

Incorporating divergent thinking exercises into daily routines can be simple and enjoyable. Creative storytelling is an activity where your child can invent new endings to familiar stories. This exercise enhances their creativity and encourages them to consider alternative perspectives. Problem-solving games, such as puzzles and strategy games, require thinking in new ways and can be a terrific way to challenge your child's mind. Open-ended questions with multiple answers also allow your child to think divergently. Questions like, "How many uses can you think of for a paperclip?" can lead to surprising and inventive ideas.

Divergent thinking isn't merely theoretical – it has real-life applications that can benefit your child in various situations. Tackling school projects with innovative approaches can lead to unique and impressive results, setting them apart from their peers. In everyday life, divergent thinking can help your child solve problems creatively, such as finding new ways to organize their room or inventing a new game to play with friends. Engaging in science experiments that encourage hypothesis testing allows them to explore different outcomes and learn from the process, instilling a love for discovery and experimentation.

**Interactive Element: Divergent Thinking Scavenger Hunt**

Try a "Divergent Thinking Scavenger Hunt" with your child. Create a list of everyday items, such as a spoon, a sock, and a cardboard box. Challenge your child to produce as many creative uses for each item as possible. This activity encourages creativity and demonstrates the value of seeing the world from different angles.

By nurturing divergent thinking skills, you empower your child to approach the world with an open mind and a thirst for innovation. These skills will serve them well in academic pursuits and life as they learn to navigate challenges creatively and confidently.

## 6.2 THE SOCRATIC METHOD: STIMULATING INTELLECTUAL CURIOSITY

Sometimes dinnertime conversations can spiral into a discussion about whether robots could ever write poetry. At times like this, instead of settling for simple *yes* or *no* answers, you and your child could engage in a dialogue that digs deep into creativity and artificial intelligence. Welcome to the Socratic Method, a cooperative dialogue that encourages critical thinking by asking and answering questions. Named after the ancient Greek philosopher Socrates, this method transforms ordinary conversations into opportunities for intellectual exploration. They don't just involve getting to the correct answer; they promote understanding why various answers might hold weight. Instead of merely scratching the surface, this technique gets into the heart of ideas, encouraging a deeper exploration of concepts.

Implementing the Socratic Method at home can open a world of intellectual curiosity for your child. Start by posing open-ended questions that require thoughtful responses. Instead of asking, "Did you like the book?" try, "What do you think the author was trying to say?" This encourages your child to think critically and express their ideas. Encourage them to ask questions and seek answers, as this develops a sense of curiosity and independence. Facilitate discussions on various topics, from ethical dilemmas to scientific theories. Consider asking, "What do you think would happen if everyone had the same amount of money?" or "Why do you think the sky is blue?" These discussions stimulate your child's mind and create a space where exploration is the goal, not just answers.

The benefits of using the Socratic Method are numerous and can profoundly impact your child's development. It enhances critical thinking and reasoning skills, pushing your child to consider different viewpoints and evaluate evidence. Encouraging active listening and respectful debate teaches them to thoughtfully engage with others' ideas, a skill that will serve them well throughout life. It also promotes self-reflection and independent thinking, helping your child develop their unique perspective on the world. By challenging assumptions and exploring possibilities, the Socratic Method enables your child to think deeply and critically, nurturing a lifelong love of learning.

Consider specific examples of Socratic questions you might use to guide these discussions. Asking, "What do you think would happen if we lived underwater?" could lead to a fascinating conversation about marine life, ecosystems, and human adaptation. "Why do you believe that is true?" encourages your child to articulate the reasoning behind their beliefs, cultivating self-awareness and critical thinking. "Can you think of another way to approach this problem?" invites them to explore alternative solutions, enhancing their critical thinking skills. Finally, "What evidence supports your answer?" teaches them to evaluate information critically and build arguments based on facts.

### *Textual Element: Socratic Dialogue Exercise*

Try a Socratic Dialogue Exercise with your child. Choose a topic of interest, such as "The Impact of Technology on Society." Over dinner, take turns asking and answering Socratic questions about the topic. This exercise encourages critical thinking and open dialogue, providing a meaningful way to explore complex issues together.

In our fast-paced world, where answers are often just a click away, the Socratic Method offers a refreshing approach to learning. It encourages exploration and discovery and nurtures a sense of wonder and curiosity in your child. By integrating this method into your daily interactions, you'll go beyond teaching them to think; you'll teach them to love thinking.

## 6.3 ENRICHMENT ACTIVITIES: BEYOND THE CLASSROOM

Picture your child, eyes wide with excitement, tinkering with a robot they built from scratch. This is the magic of enrichment activities—opportunities that stretch beyond the confines of a traditional classroom, offering gifted children the chance to delve deeper into their interests. These activities are more than optional extras; they are vital for nurturing the curiosity and talents of talented kids. By availing of these opportunities, children can explore a range of interests, enhancing their skills and expanding their knowledge in various domains. You might find that your child develops a passion for robotics, debate, or even the intricacies of chess strategies. Each activity becomes a steppingstone, encouraging them to learn, grow, and discover new talents.

There's a vast variety of enrichment activities available, offering something for all children's unique interests and abilities. Extracurricular clubs like robotics, debate, and chess provide structured environments where children can engage with peers who share their passions. These clubs often promote a sense of belonging and camaraderie, where your child can thrive alongside others who think and explore as they do. Workshops and camps offer specialized arts, sciences, and technology programs, allowing for intensive, hands-on exploration that can ignite a lifelong interest. Whether it is a summer camp focused on coding or a weekend workshop in creative writing, these experiences provide invaluable opportunities for growth and discovery. Field trips to museums, science centers, and historical sites round out options, offering real-world experiences that connect academic learning to the tangible world. Imagine your child's awe as they stand before a T-Rex skeleton or a Van Gogh painting – these are moments that can inspire and educate in ways textbooks cannot.

Selecting suitable enrichment activities for your child requires some detective work. Consider their passions and strengths, as these will guide you to programs where they will likely flourish. A child who loves building with blocks might be a natural fit for a robotics club, while a young storyteller might find their voice in a creative writing class. Balancing structured activities with free exploration is important. While courses and clubs provide valuable guidance, allowing your child to explore their interests independently can lead to some of the most profound discoveries. When evaluating programs, assess the quality and suitability of the activities and instructors. Visit facilities, speak with program leaders, and, if possible, observe a class in action. This will give you a sense of whether the environment is one where your child will feel comfortable and challenged.

Creating a home-based enrichment program can be just as effective and rewarding as doing external activities, and it often allows for more flexibility and personalization. Start by setting up a dedicated space in your home where creative projects and experiments can unfold without interruption. This might be a corner of the living room or a nook in your child's bedroom, equipped with the necessary tools and materials to explore their interests. Access to various resources is vital—books, art supplies, science kits, and musical instruments can all spark creativity and curiosity. Encourage your child to engage in self-directed learning and independent research. Whether they are reading a biography of a favorite historical figure or experimenting with a chemistry set, these activities can nurture a love of deep and enduring learning.

*Interactive Element: Enrichment Activity Planner*

Consider creating an "Enrichment Activity Planner" with your child. Sit together and brainstorm a list of activities they are interested in exploring. Then, schedule time each week for structured activities and free exploration, ensuring a balance between guidance and independence. This planner will be a useful guide for your child's educational adventures at home and beyond.

These activities are more than just idle pastimes; they allow your child to explore the world, discover their passions, and develop skills that will serve them throughout their lives. By choosing the right mix of enriching activities, you can help unlock their potential, offering them a rich variety of experiences that will inspire and challenge them in equal measure.

## 6.4 BALANCING STRUCTURE AND FREEDOM IN LEARNING

Balancing structure and freedom are essential for supporting gifted children in their learning environments. Just as a cat has its own agendas but loves home comforts, so gifted children thrive when given both a framework for progress and the freedom to explore. Structure offers the necessary support to keep them on track and help them reach their goals. However, without the freedom to explore their interests, their innate curiosity may diminish. Gifted children need the opportunity to wander intellectually, explore their passions, and discover new interests.

When creating a flexible learning environment, you need to carefully balance structure and freedom. Practically speaking, this is done by establishing a consistent routine but leaving room for spontaneous bursts of inspiration. This could look like setting aside specific times for structured study intertwined with slots for independent exploration. Set clear expectations and goals but once these have been met, allow your child to color outside the lines. Project-based learning can be the perfect recipe as it combines structured tasks with open-ended inquiry. For instance, your child might start with a topic like ancient civilizations but end up designing their society, complete with customs, laws, and a new language. This blend of direction and autonomy allows them to extend their learning beyond the confines of textbooks.

Encouraging self-directed learning cultivates intrinsic motivation as it transforms learning from a chore into an adventure. When children take ownership of their education, they are more likely to pursue their interests enthusiastically and diligently. Your role then shifts from instructor to guide, and you provide resources and support without micromanaging. This might mean helping them find books on topics they are enthusiastic about or setting up a small lab in the kitchen for their science experiments. The trick is to offer guidance while allowing them the freedom to make decisions and learn from successes and setbacks.

Evaluating progress and adjusting the balance between structure and freedom requires a keen eye and an open mind. Regular check-ins to discuss goals and achievements can provide valuable insights into what is working and what might need tweaking. These conversations don't have to be formal; they can happen over dinner or during a walk in the park. Reflect on the practical strategies and which ones fall flat and be ready to adapt based on your child's evolving needs and interests. Flexibility is your ally, allowing you to pivot and adjust ideas as your child grows and their interests change. It's a dynamic process, much like adjusting the sails on a boat to catch the right wind.

It's not always easy to get a balance between structure and freedom but with practice and patience, it will become second nature. By providing the stability of structure and the opportunity for exploration, you are equipping your child with the tools they need to thrive academically and creatively. This balance develops a love for learning that will serve them well throughout their lives, encouraging them to approach challenges with curiosity and resilience.

As your child grows used to this balanced environment, they will gain knowledge and a profound understanding of how to learn, adapt, and innovate.

# THE GIFT YOU CAN GIVE TO OTHER PARENTS

*"Gifted children are the cultural leaders of the future. It is our responsibility to ensure that their unique abilities are recognized, valued, and developed."*

— TRACY INMAN

For the parents of struggling learners, navigating the education system and finding the proper support for their child is a constant worry, and I certainly don't contend with the fact that not every child is lucky enough to get the support they need. However, it's also true that there's more in place for our struggling learners than for our gifted students. Many schools don't know how to push these children and give them the educational stimulation they need, and parents are left to make their best guesses about what they can do to support their children.

I've faced many challenges, which we're discussing in this book with my child. I don't mind telling you that it often felt like I was fighting a losing battle, especially in the beginning when I hadn't yet dedicated any severe time to researching this. More gifted children are out there than many of us realize, and their parents face the same challenges. How do we meet their educational needs? How do we help them handle their perfectionism and their strong emotions?

This book is designed to help you answer those questions and support your child with confidence, and I'd like to reach as many parents as possible. This is partly for the sake of the parents who I know are worrying and constantly questioning whether they're doing the right things, and it's partly for the children who could go on to do great things if they get the support they need right now. You can help me reach more parents like you. It's as easy as leaving a short review.

**By leaving a review of this book on Amazon, you'll show other parents where they can find the guidance they've been missing out on, and you'll help them give their children the best support they can.**

Reviews act like signposts directing people towards the resources they're looking for, and a few sentences from you can make a huge difference.

**Thank you so much for your support. You're helping gifted children everywhere reach their full potential.**

# MANAGING STRESS AND AVOIDING BURNOUT

## 7.1 CULTIVATING CALM: THE POWER OF MINDFULNESS FOR GIFTED CHILDREN

Doing everyday chores like the daily school run can be even more exhausting with a gifted child in the back seat. You may be trying to navigate the endless stream of school traffic while your child is asking questions about quantum mechanics or having a meltdown over leaving their socks at school. Their emotions can be intense and it's times like this where the benefits of mindfulness for both you and your child become evident.

Mindfulness is not just for yoga retreats and meditation gurus; it is a useful resource for helping gifted children regulate their emotional intensity, reduce anxiety, and improve focus. Your child can learn calming techniques that allow them to get through their day with a degree of serenity.

Gifted children often experience emotions on a grand scale, turning everyday frustrations into epic dramas. Mindfulness can help them manage these intense feelings. It works like a soothing balm that tempers the highs and lows. By teaching them to focus on the present moment, mindfulness reduces the whirlwind of anxiety that can sweep them away into a frenzy of "what-ifs" and "should-haves." It is akin to giving their overactive minds a pause button, allowing them to take a breath and reset. Moreover, mindfulness enhances their ability to concentrate. Training their attention will enable them to focus more effectively on tasks, reducing the scatterbrained feeling often accompanying their creativity and curiosity.

Introducing mindfulness to children might feel like trying to convince them that broccoli is as exciting as candy. Start with short, guided sessions to ease them into the practice. Five minutes of focused breathing can be a good starting point. Use age-appropriate mindfulness apps or videos that turn the practice into an engaging experience rather than a chore. These tools can transform mindfulness into a playful adventure, like a treasure hunt for inner peace. Incorporating mindfulness into daily routines is another effective strategy. Encourage your child to spend a few minutes each morning grounding themselves through simple breathing exercises. Over time, mindfulness will become as routine as brushing teeth; a small moment of calm before the day unfolds.

Many mindfulness exercises are highly suitable for children. Deep breathing exercises, like "belly breathing" or the "4-7-8 breathing" technique, can work wonders. Teach your child to inhale deeply, hold their breath, and then exhale slowly, feeling tension melt away with each breath. Body scan meditation is another great resource. Guide your child into focusing on various body parts, from their toes to the top of their head, noticing any sensations or tension they might be holding. Mindful walking can also be a delightful practice. Encourage your child to pay attention to the sensations of walking, feeling the ground beneath their feet and the rhythm of their steps. Visualization can whisk them away to a peaceful place in their mind, like a tranquil beach or a serene forest, providing a mental escape from stress.

Creating a mindful environment at home can support these practices. Designate a quiet, comfortable space where your child can retreat for mindfulness activities. It might be a cozy corner with soft cushions and calming colors, free from distractions. Encourage the whole family to participate in mindfulness practices. Making it a shared experience reinforces its importance and strengthens family bonds. Calming tools like stress balls or fidget toys can also be helpful, providing a tactile focus that enhances concentration and relaxation.

### Interactive Element: Mindfulness Journal

Try introducing the idea of a mindfulness journal to your child. After each mindfulness session, encourage them to jot down their thoughts and feelings. This practice reinforces the habit and provides a space for reflection and self-awareness. Over time, the journal becomes a guide to navigating their emotions and discovering what works best for them.

## 7.2 PHYSICAL ACTIVITY AND ITS BENEFITS

Sometimes your child probably bounces off the walls with enough energy to power a small town. Gifted children often have abundant energy, and finding an outlet for it is important. Physical activity is a remarkable stress buster, releasing endorphins that elevate mood and help regulate those intense emotions. Think of it as nature's little mood booster, bringing smiles and calm to even the most turbulent days. Exercise improves mental well-being and promotes better sleep and overall health, turning a frazzled day into a more manageable one. It is like hitting a reset button, allowing your child to unwind and recharge, ready to tackle their next intellectual challenge with renewed vigor.

Integrating physical activity into daily life does not have to be a Herculean task. Participation in sports or dance can provide a structured way for your child to burn off excess energy while learning valuable skills such as teamwork and discipline. Whether they are kicking a soccer ball or pirouetting across the living room, these activities offer a delightful blend of fun and exercise. Scheduling regular family walks or bike rides can transform exercise into a bonding experience. For instance, you could take a stroll through the park with your child, chat about their day, or dream up wild stories about the squirrels you pass. Setting up a home exercise routine can also be effective, especially on rainy days when outdoor play is not an option. A mini obstacle course in the backyard or a dance-off in the living room can turn fitness into a joyful activity rather than a chore.

When choosing the type of physical activity, consider your child's interests and personality. Team sports like soccer, basketball, or baseball can be fantastic for children who thrive on social interaction and cooperative play. These sports teach physical skills and how to work as a team, win gracefully, and lose with dignity. For those who prefer more solitary pursuits, individual activities such as swimming, running, or gymnastics offer a chance to focus on personal goals and achievements. Creative movement activities like yoga, martial arts, or dance can particularly benefit gifted children, combining physical exertion with mental focus and creativity. These activities allow children to express themselves physically while honing their concentration and discipline.

Balancing physical activity with academic and other responsibilities can be tough but creating a balanced weekly schedule can provide structure and ensure that exercise remains a priority. Consider physical activity as simply an important part of the routine, right up there with homework and piano practice. Encouraging short, frequent activity breaks during study sessions can also work wonders. A few minutes of jumping jacks or a quick jog around the block can refresh the mind and improve focus, making study time more productive and less of a slog.

The benefits of physical activity extend beyond the immediate release of energy or mood enhancement. It contributes to your child's overall well-being, nurturing a healthy body and a resilient mind. Regular exercise helps manage stress, enhances cognitive function, and builds a foundation for a lifetime of healthy habits.

## 7.3 RECOGNIZING AND ADDRESSING SIGNS OF BURNOUT

It's worrying when your gifted child, usually a whirlwind of curiosity and creativity, is suddenly transformed into a couch potato, lacking the energy to engage in their favorite activities. This could signify burnout, a standard trap for gifted kids constantly caught up in expectations and extracurriculars. Identifying burnout early is imperative, and it often manifests as chronic fatigue or a noticeable lack of energy. Your child might begin losing interest in activities they once adored, like their daily violin practice or weekend robotics club. You may notice irritability or mood swings rivaling those of teenagers and a decline in academic performance that seems out of character. These signs are the red flags, waving vigorously to alert you that something needs attention.

Burnout does not just happen overnight; it results from cumulative pressure. Overscheduling is often a prime suspect. With their myriad interests and abilities, gifted children can easily find every hour of their day packed with lessons, clubs, and competitions. This relentless pace can be overwhelming, leading to exhaustion. Add in the high personal expectations they place on themselves, often driven by perfectionism, and you have a recipe for stress or worse. Gifted kids are notorious for setting impossibly ambitious standards. When they inevitably fall short, the disappointment can weigh heavily on their minds. Moreover, a lack of downtime and relaxation exacerbates the situation. Even the most resilient child can be teetering on burnout's edge without adequate breaks.

Preventing burnout is akin to building a dam upstream. It is about taking proactive steps to ensure the pressure does not become unmanageable. Ensuring your child gets sufficient rest and sleep is a fundamental starting point. It might sound simple, but a well-rested child is far more equipped to manage stress and challenges. Setting realistic goals and expectations can also alleviate some of the pressure. Help your child understand that not every task needs to be perfect; making mistakes and learning from them is okay. Also, providing opportunities for fun and relaxation is essential. Encourage activities for enjoyment, with no strings attached, whether a silly dance party in the living room or a lazy afternoon spent building Lego castles.

What if burnout has already set in? Recognizing it is the first step and the next is thoughtful intervention. Sometimes, taking a temporary break from demanding activities can work wonders. Allow your child to step back from their commitments and recharge their batteries. This break doesn't have to be long; even a week or two can make a significant difference. Seeking support from a counselor or therapist might also be beneficial. Professional guidance can help your child understand their feelings and develop strategies to manage stress. Engaging in stress-relieving activities, such as hobbies or creative projects, provides an outlet for pent-up emotions. Whether painting, writing, or gardening, these activities allow your child to express themselves in a low-pressure environment, cultivating relaxation and joy.

Burnout results from exhaustion and from feeling overwhelmed and undervalued. Recognizing the signs early and taking steps to prevent and address them can help your child regain balance and enthusiasm. Your role as a supportive guide is essential as it ensures their brilliance continues to shine without being dimmed by the weight of expectations.

## 7.4 BALANCING ACADEMICS AND LEISURE

Sometimes your gifted child may become buried under a mountain of textbooks, cramming for yet another test, while their neglected bike collects dust in the garage. Balancing academics and leisure might seem like walking a tightrope, but it is necessary for your child's well-being. This balance prevents stress and burnout and ensures they lead a happy, satisfying life. Gifted children often have grand expectations placed on them, whether by themselves or others, which can lead to an overwhelming focus on academics. However, leisure activities are not a luxury but a necessity. Engaging in leisure helps your child reset, recharge, and return to their studies with renewed energy and creativity. This comprehensive approach to development nurtures the mind as well as the heart and soul.

Creating a balanced schedule is something you must plan consciously. Start by allocating specific times for homework, activities, and leisure. Ensuring enough time for relaxation and unstructured play is vital for letting your child's imagination run wild. Moments of spontaneous creativity are as important as any structured lesson. Regular family time should also be a staple in your schedule. It does not have to be an elaborate affair; even a simple board game night or a Sunday picnic can strengthen family bonds and provide a sense of unity and support.

Encouraging leisure activities can open a world of wonders for your child. Reading for pleasure, for example, allows them to explore different genres and authors, instilling a love for stories and ideas beyond their academic curriculum. Whether they are diving into a fantasy world or exploring historical events, reading expands their horizons in delightful ways. Creative arts, such as drawing, painting, or crafting, offer a tactile outlet for self-expression. These activities let your child create without the pressure of perfection, whether painting a masterpiece or making a collage from old magazines. Outdoor activities like hiking, gardening, or playing at the park provide a breath of fresh air, literally and figuratively. These pursuits promote physical health and connect your child with nature, offering a tranquil respite from academic pressures.

Monitoring and adjusting the balance between academics and leisure is an ongoing process. Regularly check in with your child about their feelings and stress levels. It is like taking the temperature of their emotional health. Encourage open dialogue, allowing them to express their needs and preferences. If they feel overwhelmed, be willing to change their schedule. Perhaps they need more time to unwind after school or a day off from extracurricular activities. Listen to their feedback and adjust accordingly, showing them their well-being is a priority. This adaptability teaches them that life is not a rigid script but a dynamic dance that sometimes requires a change of pace.

Balancing your child's academic and leisure hours will help cultivate a life for them that's rich with learning, love, and laughter.

You'll enable them to grow into well-rounded individuals capable of traversing life with resilience and joy.

As we turn to our next chapter, we will explore how these principles extend beyond childhood, setting the stage for lifelong success and fulfillment.

# PARENTING STRATEGIES FOR LONG-TERM SUCCESS

## 8.1 CRAFTING ATTAINABLE ASPIRATIONS: BALANCING AMBITION AND REALISM

Picture this: your child, who can recite Shakespeare while balancing on one foot, suddenly announces they will build a rocket to Mars—by Friday. As you pause to consider both the logistics and your dwindling supply of duct tape, you realize the need for setting realistic goals. Gifted children, with their boundless imagination and ambition, often dream enormously. While these grand visions are inspiring, they can also be overwhelming. Setting realistic and attainable goals is crucial to prevent unnecessary stress and burnout. When goals are realistic, they encourage steady progress and achievement, and they build self-confidence and resilience in your child. After all, the aim is to keep them climbing to new heights without falling into the abyss of frustration.

The first step in setting realistic goals is assessing your child's abilities and interests. This involves observing their strengths and identifying the areas where they excel, whether in academics, the arts, or athletics. Involving your child in the goal-setting process is vital. This empowers them to take ownership of their goals and ensures the targets align with their passions. Sit down with them and discuss what they hope to achieve, whether mastering a new skill or completing a challenging project. You are trying to build a sense of autonomy and motivation by making them active participants in this process.

Breaking down these goals into smaller, manageable tasks is the next step. It is the same principle as tackling a mountain of laundry one load at a time. Smaller tasks are less daunting and allow your child to see progress more quickly, which can be incredibly motivating. For example, if your child's goal is to draft a novel, get them started with a chapter or scene. Celebrate each completed task, reinforcing their sense of achievement and encouraging them to keep moving forward.

Balancing ambition with reality is an art form. Here, recognizing and celebrating incremental progress is helpful. Acknowledge the steps taken, not just the destinations reached, and praise the hard work and dedication to achieving a goal, regardless of the result Adjust goals as needed based on your child's development. As they grow and change, their interests and abilities will, too. Be flexible and open to revising goals to ensure they remain relevant and challenging. Regular monitoring and evaluation of goals are essential to keep your child on track and motivated. Set up regular check-ins to discuss progress and any challenges they might face. These discussions provide an opportunity to offer support and guidance, reinforcing your role as their cheerleader and coach. Visual tools like charts or planners can be a fun and effective way to track achievements. These tools provide a tangible representation of progress, making it easier for your child to see how far they have come. Adjust goals based on feedback and new insights. As your child progresses, encourage them to reflect on what they have learned and how they might approach future challenges differently.

***Interactive Element: Goal-Setting Reflection Exercise***

Your child might enjoy keeping a goal journal. After each milestone, show them how to write about what they learned, any challenges they faced, and how they overcame them. This reflection helps reinforce the skills and strategies they are developing and provides a record of their achievements to look back on with pride. If they use a notes app on their phones for this, they could include photos of their projects.

## 8.2 ENCOURAGING A GROWTH MINDSET

Imagine your child facing a tricky puzzle and declaring, "I can't do it ... yet." That is the beauty of a growth mindset, where "yet" becomes a powerful word. A growth mindset is the belief that abilities and intelligence are not fixed; they can grow with effort and learning. This mindset is essential for gifted children because it promotes resilience and a love for challenges, teaching them that their talents can be cultivated through dedication and hard work. When talented children embrace this type of mindset, they learn to see obstacles as opportunities for growth rather than insurmountable hurdles. This shift in perspective can make all the difference in how they approach their academic and personal lives and save them a lot of frustration.

Teaching growth mindset principles to your child involves focusing on effort and perseverance rather than innate talent. Praise them for their challenging work done to solve a problem, not just for getting the correct answer. This helps them understand that success results from persistence and learning rather than some magical gift they were born with. Encourage your child to embrace challenges and learn from failures, treating setbacks as valuable lessons. When they stumble, remind them that every great inventor or artist faced countless failures before achieving success. Use growth mindset language, such as adding "yet" to their self-doubts, to instill a sense of potential and possibility. For instance, when they say, "I can't play this piece of music," remind them to say instead, "I can't play this piece yet."

As parents, you play a vital role in modeling a growth mindset through your behavior. Share personal stories of overcoming challenges, letting your child see that even adults face obstacles and learn from them. Whether learning a new skill or managing a tricky situation, your experiences can be powerful examples of growth and resilience. Demonstrate a willingness to learn and grow by tackling new challenges together. Show your child that making mistakes is a natural part of learning and that perfection is neither necessary nor realistic. By embracing imperfections, you create an environment where your child feels safe to take risks and explore new possibilities without fear of judgment or failure.

Activities that support a growth mindset can be both fun and educational. Again, journalling is useful here as your child can reflect on their personal growth and achievements. They'll be able to track their progress, recognize their strengths, and identify areas for improvement. Engaging in activities that require persistence, like learning a musical instrument or a new sport, can be particularly effective. These pursuits require dedication, practice, and a willingness to push through challenges, reinforcing the growth mindset principles. Reading books and stories about characters with a growth mindset can also be inspiring. Stories of individuals who overcame adversity and achieved greatness through determination can motivate your child to adopt the same attitude.

In a world where gifted children often feel pressured to excel effortlessly, nurturing a growth mindset gives them the tools to embrace challenges with courage and curiosity. By teaching them that their potential is not fixed, you empower them to explore their abilities and develop the resilience needed to thrive in any endeavor they choose.

## 8.3 PREPARING FOR COLLEGE AND CAREER CHOICES

Navigating the world of college and career choices for your gifted child can feel like assembling a 1,000-piece puzzle with no picture on the box. You must start exploring different fields of interest early and understand the requirements for various college programs. Gifted children often have a myriad of passions, from biochemistry to avant-garde music composition, and early preparation allows them to explore these interests without the pressure of last-minute decisions. Get them to dip their toes into different career paths through summer programs or workshops, helping them identify what excites them. Involvement in extracurricular activities that align with their interests can provide invaluable experience and enhance their college applications. Whether joining the debate team or volunteering at a local science center, these activities develop skills and demonstrate commitment to their passions.

Regarding the college application process, research is your best friend. Start by investigating a range of colleges and universities to find those that offer programs suited to your child's aspirations and strengths. Each institution has its flavor, from intense research universities to liberal arts colleges focusing on holistic education. Standardized tests like the SAT or ACT are useful too but provide practice tests and prep courses to help your child familiarize themselves with the format and content.

Crafting compelling personal statements and essays is important. Urge your child to tell their unique story, showcasing their individuality, resilience, and passion. These essays are more than just writing samples—they are a chance for your child to connect with admissions officers personally.

Career exploration and planning are ongoing processes that require both introspection and action. By arranging job shadowing or internship opportunities, you can give your child a first-hand glimpse into potential careers. These experiences build skills and help them understand the day-to-day realities of different professions. Encourage your child to conduct informational interviews with professionals in fields of interest. This simple act of reaching out and asking questions can yield insights and connections. Utilize career assessment tools to identify your child's strengths and preferences. These tools can guide them toward careers that align with their skills and passions, providing direction during what can sometimes feel like an overwhelming period of exploration.

Balancing academics with life skills development is a delicate act but one that is indispensable for long-term success. Teaching financial literacy and budgeting prepares them for the practicalities of adult life, ensuring they can confidently manage their finances. Encourage independent living skills, such as cooking and time management, to generate self-reliance and resourcefulness. These skills teach them how to survive and thrive in a complex world.

Promoting social skills and networking is equally important. Encourage your child to nurture relationships and build a network of peers and mentors who can support them. Social skills are the glue that holds academic and career success together, enabling your child to traverse the nuances of professional and personal interactions easily.

## 8.4 LIFELONG LEARNING: INSTILLING A LOVE FOR KNOWLEDGE

Your child is like a sponge, soaking up information with the eagerness of youth. Nurturing a love for lifelong learning is vital for gifted children because it keeps their intellectual curiosity alive. This continuous craving for knowledge fuels their personal growth and prepares them for the ever-evolving demands of the professional world. As their interests change and develop, a mindset oriented towards lifelong learning empowers them to adapt and embrace new challenges.

To cultivate this love, create a learning environment that encourages exploration. Start by providing access to diverse resources, such as books, online courses, and workshops. Whether it is a book on quantum physics or a pottery class, these resources offer your child a buffet of intellectual delights. Encourage them to explore new hobbies and interests, no matter how obscure or unrelated they might seem. This broadens their horizons and develops a culture of curiosity at home. Make your house a place where questions are welcomed and celebrated and where the pursuit of knowledge is as natural as breathing.

As a parent, you can model a commitment to lifelong learning. Engage in your own learning pursuits and share these experiences with your child. Whether learning a new language or attending a lecture series on medieval history, your enthusiasm can be contagious. Attend classes, lectures, or seminars alongside your children, showing them that learning is a lifelong endeavor that does not stop at adulthood. Demonstrate a passion for knowledge and growth, showing your child that the world is full of wonders to explore and understand.

Encouraging self-directed learning in your child is like handing them the reins to their education. Allow them to choose their learning projects and goals and pursue what captivates their interest. Your role is to provide them with the tools and resources necessary for independent research, whether it is a trip to the library or access to online databases. You can also encourage critical thinking and problem-solving by posing open-ended questions and challenging them to find solutions. This approach will build their confidence and equip them with the skills needed to navigate life's complexities.

### Interactive Element: Curiosity Challenge

Introduce a curiosity challenge where your child picks a new topic each month to explore. Guide them toward good books, documentaries, or online courses related to the subject. At the end of the month, have them creatively present what they have learned, like a mini–TED Talk. Alternatively, they could make a scrapbook about it. This will reinforce their learning and hone their presentation skills.

This chapter has explored how cultivating a love for lifelong learning equips gifted children with the tools to thrive in an ever-changing world. As they embrace the joy of discovery, they develop intellectual prowess, resilience, and adaptability. Each new piece of knowledge becomes a steppingstone to future growth. Next, we'll explore financial planning and resources, ensuring you have the practical tools to support your child's educational journey.

# FINANCIAL PLANNING AND RESOURCES

## 9.1 STRATEGIC FINANCIAL PLANNING FOR EDUCATIONAL OPPORTUNITIES

It can be very disillusioning to have a gifted child with an appetite for learning yet not have the resources to support their needs. When considering enrichment programs for your gifted child, such as science camps, math clubs, and art workshops, it's essential to plan strategically to manage the associated costs. Balancing your child's educational aspirations with financial responsibilities requires careful budgeting and creativity. This section will explore effective strategies for financing specialized programs while ensuring that your child can access valuable learning opportunities.

Supporting your child's educational and enrichment needs starts with understanding the importance of financial planning. With the cost of private college education averaging around $41,540 per year, many parents share your concerns, with 64% actively saving or planning for their children's college education.

Begin by assessing your family's income and expenses. Identify areas where you can prioritize spending based on your child's educational needs and your family's long-term goals. Setting aside funds for academic purposes can be satisfying but stressful. Whether for tuition, materials, or educational trips, having a dedicated fund ensures you are prepared for those opportunities that can shape your child's future.

Creating a detailed budget for specialized programs does not have to be a Herculean task. Start by listing all potential expenses, including tuition, supplies, and travel associated with various programs. Estimate these costs realistically, considering factors like frequency and duration. Allocate a portion of your family budget to cover these expenses. We say, "a portion" because you can't allow your gifted child's expenses to take priority over the needs of other family members. Use spreadsheets or budgeting apps to track your financial commitments – they'll help to keep everything organized and accessible.

Long-term financial planning is the key to ensuring ongoing support for your child's education. Consider opening a dedicated savings account for educational expenses as this will allow you to separate those funds from everyday spending. The power of compound interest can work wonders over time, much like a snowball growing as it rolls down a hill. Explore investment options that align with your risk tolerance and financial goals, aiming to increase your savings steadily. Keep an eye on future costs, such as college tuition, and plan accordingly. Setting realistic savings goals and utilizing tax-advantaged accounts like 529 plans or Roth IRAs can make a significant difference. Remember to also prioritize your retirement savings alongside your child's education savings—after all, there are no scholarships for retirement.

Adjusting and monitoring your budget is vital to staying on track. Regularly review your expenses and compare them to your budget to identify discrepancies. Adjust based on changes in family income, needs, or educational goals. There are plenty of budgeting tools and apps available to simplify this process for you, transforming fiscal management from a daunting task into a routine check-up. Involve your child in financial discussions if you feel it's appropriate to teach them about the valuable life skills of budgeting and saving. Maintaining a flexible approach and updating your plan as needed will enable you to support your gifted child's educational journey while maintaining your family's financial stability.

### *Interactive Element: Budgeting Reflection Exercise*

Consider engaging in a budgeting reflection exercise with your child. Discuss their educational goals and dreams, then collaboratively outline the associated costs. Reflect on how your family can prioritize and adjust spending to support their aspirations. This exercise cultivates financial literacy and reinforces the value of thoughtful planning.

## 9.2 FINDING SCHOLARSHIPS AND GRANTS

Imagine your child's face lighting up at the thought of attending a prestigious summer program or a specialized school. Then, reality hits like a splash of chilly water when considering the costs. Don't worry, scholarships and grants can make these dreams attainable without draining your savings. The trick lies in researching and identifying these opportunities. Start with online databases and scholarship search engines. These digital troves are invaluable, offering filters to match your child's talents and needs with available funds. Checking with local educational institutions and organizations is also helpful. Schools often know about scholarships and grants catering to local students and might even offer their own. Networking with other parents and educators can uncover even more opportunities. A casual chat at a PTA meeting could lead to discovering a scholarship that perfectly aligns with your child's interests and achievements.

Scholarships and grants come in various flavors, each with its own criteria. Merit-based scholarships reward academic achievements, talents, or skills. They are like gold stars for your child's hard work and dedication. Need-based grants consider your family's financial situation, providing support where needed. Program-specific scholarships target subjects or fields, perfect for the budding scientist or aspiring artist in your home. Community-based scholarships come from local organizations or groups, often focusing on supporting students within the community. These are particularly valuable, as they provide financial aid while instilling a sense of regional pride and support for your child's educational journey.

The application process for scholarships and grants can be arduous. It requires organization, attention to detail, and persistence. Start by gathering necessary documents, such as transcripts and recommendation letters. These are your child's academic résumé, displaying their brilliance and achievements. Write compelling personal statements or essays. Help your child to tell their story, highlighting their passions, goals, and the impact they hope to make. It is their chance to shine and let their personality leap off the page. Meeting application deadlines is non-negotiable. Create a timeline to track due dates and follow up on submissions to ensure everything is in order.

Maximizing the chances of securing scholarships and grants involves a strategic approach. Encourage your child to apply to multiple opportunities, casting their net wide to begin with. It's important to customize applications to fit each scholarship's specific criteria. It's not good enough to simply send off a generic document. Highlight your child's unique achievements and experiences that align with the scholarship's focus. This tailored approach demonstrates a genuine connection between your child's goals and the scholarship's mission. Persevere and your child's educational aspirations can become a reality.

***Textual Element: Scholarship Application Checklist***

Consider creating a scholarship application checklist with your child. This tool can help them organize their applications, ensuring they gather all necessary documents, craft compelling essays, and meet deadlines. It will provide a practical guide to navigating the scholarship process, turning a daunting task into a manageable and rewarding endeavor.

## 9.3 COST-EFFECTIVE ENRICHMENT ACTIVITIES

Imagine discovering a bunch of enriching activities for your gifted child without needing a map—or a hefty budget. You're basically looking for cost-effective options that deliver valuable experiences, ensuring your child continues to thrive intellectually and creatively. Start by exploring local community centers, which often offer a variety of classes and workshops at a fraction of the cost of private programs. From dance and art to coding and chess, these centers can be a goldmine for discovering new interests. Also, don't underestimate online courses and virtual learning platforms; they provide flexible learning opportunities right from your living room. Whether it is a course on creative writing or a deep dive into astrophysics, these resources can keep your child's mind engaged without requiring a second mortgage. Free or low-cost extracurricular clubs and organizations in your area can also offer enriching experiences. Check local bulletin boards or community websites to find groups that align with your child's interests and talents.

For those days when you are feeling particularly adventurous—or when the weather traps you indoors, DIY enriching activities at home can be economical and incredibly fun. You put your kitchen into a laboratory or your dining table into an art workshop. A set of cheap watercolors and some paper can open a world of creativity. Get your child to create a masterpiece inspired by their favorite artist or a scene from their latest book. Alternatively, explore drawing with different mediums like charcoal or shoe polish. Educational games and puzzles are another fantastic way to keep young minds sharp without splurging on expensive toys. Dust off those old board games or download free educational apps that make learning feel like playtime.

Public resources are often free and may surprise you with what they have available. Public libraries, often the unsung education heroes, offer more than books. Many host workshops, events, and even clubs specifically designed for children. Whether it is a storytelling session or a craft workshop, these events provide many learning opportunities. Libraries often loan out more than books too; check if they also lend educational kits or games. Local parks and nature reserves are perfect for outdoor learning. They offer a hands-on experience with nature that cannot be replicated in a classroom. Whether identifying local flora and fauna or understanding ecosystems, these outings are rich in educational value. Keep an eye out for free community events and cultural festivals that will offer your child an immersive experience in diverse cultures and traditions while having fun.

Speaking of community, bartering and skill swapping with other parents is another creative way to access enrichment activities.

What about trading tutoring or skill lessons with other parents? You might be a whiz at math, while your neighbor may be a talented musician. Swap lessons and watch as your children gain new skills while you save money. Organizing group activities where each parent contributes a different skill can also be enriching. One parent might lead a science experiment while another teaches an art class. Creating a community network for shared resources and support broadens educational horizons and builds a sense of camaraderie among families. By pooling resources and expertise, you can make an enriching, diverse, affordable, and enriching environment for your child.

## 9.4 UTILIZING COMMUNITY RESOURCES

It should be quite easy to find and utilize community programs to support your gifted child. Local museums and science center's often offer educational programs tailored for curious minds. These institutions provide workshops, camps, and events that allow your child to explore subjects like marine biology or robotics in depth. Imagine your child's eyes widening as they peer through a microscope for the first time or program a robot to dance!

Community colleges and universities frequently have youth outreach programs. These initiatives can range from weekend classes to summer camps, providing a collegiate atmosphere that can inspire your child to aim high. Non-profit organizations dedicated to education also offer a wealth of enrichment opportunities. These groups often provide scholarships or free access to programs, ensuring financial constraints do not limit your child's potential.

Building a support network within the community can be a lifeline for parents of gifted children. Joining parent support groups allows you to share experiences, advice, and sometimes even a much-needed laugh over your shared challenges. These groups can be found through schools, libraries, or online platforms and often host regular meetings or social events. Connecting with local educators and specialists can also be valuable. These professionals can provide insights into your child's academic needs and offer guidance on available resources. Participating in community forums and online groups expands your network, providing access to a broader range of perspectives and experiences.

Leveraging public services for educational support is another way to enrich your child's learning experience. Libraries and community centers frequently offer free tutoring programs, often staffed by volunteers or college students eager to help. These resources provide personalized support that can complement your child's schoolwork. Public transportation can be a convenient way to access educational programs and events, especially in various parts of the city. Many cities offer students discounted or free passes, making exploring new opportunities easier. Government-funded programs and initiatives can also provide significant support. These programs might include grants for educational materials or funding for special projects, and they are often designed to ensure equal access to educational opportunities for all students.

Volunteering and giving back enriches your child's education and instills a sense of social responsibility. Volunteering at local organizations or events can provide hands-on learning experiences. Whether helping at a wildlife sanctuary or participating in a community clean-up, these activities teach valuable skills and foster a sense of accomplishment. Engaging in community service projects can also help your child build connections with peers and mentors who share their interests. Encouraging your child to participate in these activities shows them the importance of giving back and contributing to their community. Teaching children the value of social responsibility can be as simple as discussing the impact of their volunteer work over dinner, helping them see how their actions make a difference.

As we wrap up this chapter, we want to emphasize that community resources offer many opportunities to support your gifted child's development. Whether through volunteering or connecting with local experts, these community connections can profoundly enrich your child's life.

# 10

# PARENTAL SELF-CARE AND SUPPORT

Parenting a gifted child can be a demanding experience, characterized by an endless stream of questions, emotional fluctuations, and educational challenges. Amidst these daily responsibilities, finding time for self-care often feels difficult. However, effective time management can help you carve out space for your well-being while supporting your child's needs.

## 10.1 TIME MANAGEMENT FOR PARENTS

First, it is important to identify priorities, as not all tasks on your to-do list hold the same urgency. The Eisenhower Matrix is a useful tool for sorting tasks by urgency and importance. This matrix categorizes tasks into four groups: urgent and important (such as addressing a child's immediate needs), important but not urgent (like planning a family vacation), urgent but not essential (such as responding to an email about a non-critical meeting), and neither urgent nor essential (like reorganizing your sock drawer). By categorizing tasks, you can concentrate on what truly matters and what can be postponed.

Creating a balanced schedule is essential for effective time management. Begin by blocking out time for work, family, and personal activities, ensuring that you include self-care. Utilize digital calendars or planners to organize your day as they are great for helping you keep track of tasks and appointments. A well-structured schedule allows for more intentional time management, reducing the feeling of constantly rushing and enabling you to dedicate moments to self-care, whether through a quiet cup of tea or a short walk.

Delegating tasks is not a sign of weakness but a savvy parenting strategy. Assign age-appropriate chores to your children, turning them into valuable contributors to the household. Suddenly, setting the table or tidying up toys becomes an exciting mission rather than a chore. If your budget allows, consider hiring help for household tasks. Imagine the luxury of coming home to a clean house without lifting a finger! Outsourcing specific responsibilities can free up time, allowing you to focus on what truly matters: being present and engaged with your family.

Setting boundaries is your shield against the relentless tide of demands. Designate specific times for work and family activities, creating a clear separation between professional obligations and personal time. This boundary will act like a moat, protecting your precious personal time from being overrun by work-related responsibilities. Remember – it is okay to say no to non-essential commitments. You do not have to bake two hundred cupcakes for the school fair or join every committee. Saying *no* allows you to focus your energy on what helps you grow.

### *Interactive Element: Time Management Quiz*

Consider taking a short quiz to assess your current time management skills. Reflect on your answers and identify areas where you might improve. This exercise can provide insights into how you allocate your time and where adjustments could be made to balance your personal and family life better.

Effective time management is not just a tool but a lifeline in the whirlwind of parenting. By prioritizing tasks, creating a balanced schedule, delegating responsibilities, and setting boundaries, you *can* carve out time for self-care and reclaim control. Keep in mind that you cannot pour from an empty cup. So, grab that planner and schedule some "me time."

## 10.2 SEEKING SUPPORT NETWORKS

You have just spent an hour explaining to your child why Pluto is no longer classified as a planet, only to be met with a barrage of questions that would stump even the most seasoned astronomer. Moments like this underscore the importance of having a support network. Parenting a gifted child can be a lonely road, punctuated by moments of triumph, frustration, and exhaustion that others might not fully grasp. This is where a solid support network becomes invaluable as an emotional safety net. These are the people who understand the unique challenges and joys you face, reducing feelings of isolation and providing practical advice drawn from shared experiences.

Building a personal support system adds warmth and comfort to a sometimes-lonely road. Start by regularly connecting with friends and family members. These people know you best and can offer a listening ear or a helping hand when needed. They might not understand every intricacy of giftedness, but they can provide the emotional support that is so necessary. Grandparents and other extended family members can be particularly helpful. They often bring a wealth of experience and wisdom to the table, offering a different perspective on parenting challenges. Their involvement can provide additional emotional support and a sense of stability for both you and your child. Whether it's sharing stories of their own parenting journeys or simply being available to lend a hand, their presence can alleviate some of the stress associated with raising a gifted child. They may even be willing to make a weekly time when your child can visit, thereby giving you a bit of time for yourself.

Do not hesitate to seek professional support from therapists or counselors if you feel overwhelmed. Professionals can offer guidance and strategies tailored to your family's needs, helping you navigate the complexities of raising a gifted child.

Check with schools, community centers, and local organizations. Many of these places host support groups specifically for parents of gifted children. Schools are often a good starting point, as teachers and administrators can connect you with other parents, navigating similar waters. Local community centers may offer parenting workshops or support groups tailored to the needs of gifted children. These gatherings provide a space to share stories, swap strategies, and lend an empathetic ear when needed.

Do not overlook the power of online platforms, either. A quick search can turn up forums and groups where parents exchange tips, triumphs, and even the occasional meme about the trials of raising a mini genius. Online communities and forums are a lifeline for many parents. They offer a vast pool of wisdom and camaraderie that can be accessed from the comfort of your home. Platforms like Facebook host groups dedicated to parenting gifted children, where you can engage in discussions and seek advice from parents who have been there and done that. These forums often buzz with activity, offering various perspectives, from educational resources to managing emotional intensity. They are a place to pose questions, share victories, or vent about your child's latest escapade. And the best part? You can do all this in your pajamas, coffee in hand, while your child conducts their latest science experiment in the next room.

***Textual Element: Support Network Reflection Section***

Take a moment to reflect on your current support network. Think about who you turn to when you need advice or encouragement. Are there gaps in your network that you would like to fill? Use this time of reflection to jot down potential sources of support, whether local groups, online communities, or personal connections.

## 10.3 MAINTAINING MENTAL AND PHYSICAL HEALTH

As the primary support for your family, managing the various aspects of daily life can be demanding, especially when also addressing the unique challenges of raising a gifted child. You must prioritize your mental and physical health, as your well-being directly impacts your ability to support your child effectively. Maintaining good health is not merely a luxury; it is vital for reducing stress and preventing burnout. By taking care of yourself, you'll ensure you can provide the stability and support your child and other family members need.

Let's start with mental health. Think of it as the foundation on which all your parenting superpowers rest. Regular mindfulness and meditation can work wonders, helping you clear your mind of the endless to-do lists and worries that can pile up like laundry. Taking just a few minutes each day to breathe deeply or practice guided meditation can leave you feeling refreshed and grounded, ready to tackle the day. But don't stop there; carve out time for hobbies and activities that bring you joy. Whether painting, gardening, or getting lost in an enjoyable book, these moments of personal fulfillment are like oxygen for your soul. And if life feels overwhelming, don't hesitate to seek **regular therapy or counseling**. A professional can offer guidance and strategies to help you navigate the complexities of **parenting a gifted child with confidence** and clarity of purpose.

Physical health is equally important, as it gives you the stamina to power through your daily activities. You don't have to spend hours in the gym – incorporate physical activity into your routine, whether it is a brisk walk in the morning, a yoga session before bed, or a quick dance party in the living room with your kids. Exercise releases endorphins, those magical chemicals that boost your mood and energy levels. Pair this with a balanced diet and stay hydrated and you'll be set up for success. Remember, you are feeding your body and fueling your ability to face the day with vitality.

Let's not forget the importance of adequate sleep and rest. Your body's natural reset button, sleep, is indispensable for maintaining both physical health and mental acuity.

Creating a self-care routine is like crafting a personalized wellness plan. Designate specific times each day for self-care activities, treating them as non-negotiable appointments with yourself. These might include a morning meditation, an afternoon stroll, or an evening soak in the bath. To ensure consistency, create a self-care checklist. Jot down activities that rejuvenate you and check them off as you go. This is as a reminder and a motivator, helping you stay on track even when life gets hectic. Incorporating relaxation techniques, such as reading or bathing, can provide a soothing escape from the day's demands.

Maintaining mental and physical health is not an extravagance but it serves to fortify your well-being so you can be the parent your child needs. By prioritizing self-care, you'll enhance your quality of life and set a powerful example for your child, teaching them the value of caring for themselves.

## 10.4 BALANCING FAMILY DYNAMICS

Picture your household as a bustling orchestra, each family member playing their unique instrument. Understanding each member's roles and needs is central to creating harmony. In families with gifted children, the dynamics can resemble a symphony, with high notes of creativity and deep undertones of emotion. Acknowledging everyone's unique needs helps create a supportive, collaborative environment where everyone feels valued. Your gifted child might be the soloist, drawing much of your attention with their astonishing abilities and relentless curiosity. Meanwhile, siblings might feel like they're playing second fiddle and yearning for the spotlight. Recognizing these dynamics allows you to address them, ensuring every child feels seen, heard, and valued.

Open communication is the conductor's baton that keeps this orchestra in sync. Family meetings offer a platform to discuss concerns, plans, and triumphs. These gatherings do not have to be formal – consider a casual catch-up over pizza, for example. Encourage active listening where each member gets to the floor to share their thoughts while others listen with empathy. Such gatherings are a chance to practice conflict resolution techniques, transforming disagreements into opportunities for growth. This approach strengthens bonds and teaches invaluable communication skills.

Ensuring equal attention is given to all the children is essential for maintaining a balance within the family. Scheduling one-on-one time with each child helps nurture personal connections, away from the distractions of daily life. You could, for example, take each child separately out for a milkshake and special time with Mum or Dad. It's important to celebrate each child's achievements, whether it's a good test score or a creative project. Avoid making comparisons between siblings, and instead focus on promoting individuality. For instance, while Mike may be brilliant at math, Rebecca is a wonderful young artist, and Peter is an amazing cook. This approach helps each child recognize their unique worth and contribution to the family.

Family traditions and rituals are the glue that binds your family together. Regular activities like game nights or outings create a sense of belonging and offer moments of joy to look forward to. These traditions, whether Saturday morning pancake breakfasts or annual camping trips, become cherished memories. Celebrate holidays and special occasions together, making them opportunities for connection and reflection. Simple daily or weekly rituals, like bedtime stories or Sunday afternoon walks, can strengthen family bonds. These shared experiences weave a tapestry of togetherness, providing a comforting backdrop to the hustle and bustle of everyday life.

Balancing family dynamics is an ongoing process in the grand scheme of parenting a gifted child. It is about recognizing each family member's unique contributions and creating an environment where everyone thrives. You nurture a family that supports and uplifts each other by fostering open communication, ensuring equal attention, and building traditions. As we explore these dynamics, remember that every family is a work in progress, continuously evolving and growing together.

# 11

# REAL-LIFE CASE STUDIES AND EXAMPLES

Attending a school meeting to advocate for their child's grade advancement can be a challenging experience for many parents of gifted children. With these children, advocacy often becomes a significant responsibility, requiring parents to promote their child's needs actively. In this role, you may find yourself serving as an advocate, supporter, and sometimes even a legal representative. Fortunately, experienced parents who have been through this process successfully can offer valuable insights and strategies to help you advocate effectively for your child.

## 11.1 SUCCESSFUL ADVOCACY STORIES

Let's start with the tale of the Johnson family, who faced a school system reluctant to accelerate their son, Alex. The school hesitated despite Alex's ability to calculate *pi* to the nth decimal place and his insatiable thirst for learning. They feared social ramifications and questioned whether he was truly ready. Undeterred, the Johnsons gathered a portfolio showcasing Alex's academic prowess, including test scores and teacher recommendations. They met with school officials armed with evidence, not just enthusiasm. Their persistence paid off when Alex was placed in an accelerated program where he thrived academically and socially. The lesson here? Persistence and evidence-based advocacy can move mountains—or school policies.

In another inspiring tale, the Smiths faced the challenge of securing an Individualized Education Plan (IEP) for their twice-exceptional daughter, Lily. Lily's brilliance in art was matched only by her struggles with dyslexia. The Smiths realized Lucy's dual needs early on, but the school initially viewed Lily's challenges as hurdles rather than components of her unique learning profile. The Smiths collaborated closely with educators and specialists, emphasizing federal mandates for comprehensive assessments to address Lily's educational needs. They tailored an IEP that included academic goals and accommodations like assistive technology. The outcome was remarkable: Lily's academic performance improved and her confidence soared, proving the power of customized support and collaboration.

Then there is the story of the Taylors, who opted to homeschool their gifted and highly inquisitive son, Ethan. Traditional classrooms did not fit; they were like squeezing a square peg into a round hole. The Taylors weighed the pros and cons, considering Ethan's need for individualized attention and a curriculum tailored to his pace. They designed a personalized learning plan incorporating his love for science and history. They also found social opportunities through homeschooling networks, ensuring Ethan developed social skills alongside his academic talents. The results spoke for themselves—Ethan's academic performance flourished, and he became a well-rounded, confident individual.

Lastly, meet the Gonzalez family, who embarked on a quest to find a specialized program for their daughter, Sofia, whose talent in mathematics was as dazzling as a firework display. They researched extensively and finally identified a program that matched Sofia's abilities and interests. The application process was rigorous and involved essays, interviews, and a fair amount of nail-biting. However, Sofia's transition to the new program was smooth, thanks to the resources and intellectual peers she found there. The reasons were clear: Sofia had access to advanced coursework that fed her curiosity and sparked her enthusiasm for learning.

## 11.2 OVERCOMING EMOTIONAL CHALLENGES

Emotional challenges often feel like an uninvited guest in the homes of families with gifted children, lingering long after the party has ended. Take the Reynolds family, who noticed that their son, Jake, was increasingly frustrated by the slightest mistakes in his schoolwork. His perfectionism was like a shadow that followed him everywhere and cast doubt on his abilities. Reynolds decided enough was enough and implemented growth mindset strategies, encouraging Jake to see mistakes as learning opportunities rather than failures. They introduced mindfulness techniques, such as deep breathing and visualization, to help Jake manage anxiety. A school counselor joined the team, providing a safe space for Jake to express his worries and work through them. Over time, Jake's anxiety lessened, and his resilience grew stronger, much like a young sapling becoming a sturdy tree.

The Thompsons faced a different emotional hurdle with their daughter, Emily, whose emotions resembled a rollercoaster with no safety bar. Her frequent outbursts and heightened sensitivity left the family in a constant state of alert. They approached the situation with emotional coaching, helping Emily identify and articulate her feelings. They also created a calming environment at home, with a cozy nook filled with her favorite books and soft music to soothe her nerves. Consulting with a child psychologist provided additional insight and techniques for Emily to regulate her emotions better. As weeks turned into months, Emily's ability to cope with her feelings improved, and the rollercoaster ride began to smooth out, offering more gentle curves and fewer dramatic drops.

Meanwhile, the Lees grappled with their daughter Sophia's sense of social isolation. Sophia often felt misunderstood and struggled to connect with her peers and make lasting friendships. Recognizing the need for change, the Lees enrolled her in clubs that piqued her interests, such as a local art class and a robotics group. They also arranged playdates with children who shared similar passions. Teaching Sophia social skills and empathy became a family effort, with each member contributing to role-playing exercises and discussions about emotions. Slowly but surely, Sophia's social interactions improved, and she began forming meaningful friendships, proving that with patience and the proper support, even the most isolated child can find their place in the world.

The Garcias, conversely, discovered their son's emotional resilience was more like a house of cards, toppling at the slightest breeze of adversity. They observed patterns of giving up quickly, especially when faced with challenging tasks. Determined to help him build a stronger foundation, they turned to positive reinforcement and activities designed to build resilience. From celebrating small victories to engaging in family discussions about overcoming challenges, they created an environment that nurtured growth and perseverance. As their son learned to tackle setbacks with a newfound sense of determination, his ability to manage life's ups and downs was transformed, becoming a solid fortress capable of weathering any storm.

## 11.3 BALANCING ACADEMICS AND SOCIAL LIFE

The Williams family was always on the go, their calendars bursting with color-coded entries for Max's violin lessons, math club, and soccer practice. Initially, the flurry of activities seemed like a great idea—after all, keeping their gifted son engaged was a top priority. However, they soon realized that the constant rush was taking a toll. Max was stressed, and the family hardly ever shared a meal. The solution began with a family meeting where everyone aired their grievances and wishes. They prioritized activities that mattered, cutting back on the essentials Max loved most. Digital calendars became their best friends, and Sunday evenings became planning sessions. The result was a more balanced daily life with space for spontaneity and the occasional lazy afternoon. Max's stress levels dropped, and the family connections strengthened, proving that sometimes less is more.

Then there are the Parkers, who faced a different challenge. Their daughter, Lily, was hesitant to join extracurricular activities, fearing they would interfere with her academics. Yet, they understood the importance of social skills and broader interests for her growth. The Parkers decided to uncover Lily's hidden passions. They explored everything from pottery to coding, finally striking gold with a local theater group. Setting clear boundaries for homework time ensured that her studies did not suffer. They became her most prominent cheerleaders, attending performances and providing transportation. As Lily's confidence grew, so did her circle of friends and interests, transforming her into a well-rounded individual with a zest for life beyond textbooks.

The Taylors, like many parents, noticed their son, Jeremy, was crumbling under the weight of academic pressure. His once bright eyes dulled with every mention of schoolwork, and anxiety crept in like an uninvited guest. Realizing the need for intervention, the

Taylors introduced stress management techniques, like deep breathing and journaling, into Jeremy's routine. They also collaborated with his teachers to adjust his workload, ensuring it was challenging yet manageable. Jeremy learned to set realistic goals and celebrate small victories, which reduced his stress and reignited his love for learning. The transformation was gradual but profound, like watching a wilting plant revive under the care of a dedicated gardener.

Finally, we meet the Garcias, who embraced the idea that play is as vital as academics. Their daughter, Sofia, thrived on structure yet craved the freedom to explore without constraints. The Garcias recognized the importance of downtime, understanding that play is not just a break from learning but an important part of development. They scheduled regular playdates and family outings, creating a family calendar with designated leisure time that became sacred. The result was a happier, more relaxed Sofia who bonded with her family and friends. Her mood improved, and the family enjoyed shared adventures and simple pleasures, like a weekend hike or an afternoon baking cupcakes.

## 11.4 DIVERSE EXPERIENCES: VOICES FROM DIFFERENT BACKGROUNDS

Consider the Ahmed family, who moved to a new country so their bright daughter, Layla, could access better educational opportunities. Balancing their cultural expectations with Layla's giftedness was no small feat. Her parents found themselves trying to decipher a new educational system, trying to maintain their cultural values while embracing Layla's academic potential. They faced challenges as they searched for resources that respected their heritage and Layla's needs. Luckily, they discovered a culturally relevant support group that connected them with other families in similar situations. Through shared experiences and advice, they learned to integrate their values with their educational goals. This adaptation allowed Layla to thrive academically and helped her parents remain anchored in their cultural identity. Layla's success story is a testament to the power of community and the importance of finding a support system that honors one's cultural roots.

Meanwhile, the Rodriguez family faced different hurdles. Living in a community with limited financial resources, they struggled to provide their gifted son, Miguel, with access to enrichment activities and specialized programs. The cost of these opportunities seemed impossibly high at first. Determined to support Miguel's talents, they tapped into local community resources and applied for scholarships. They found unexpected allies in local organizations that offered low-cost or free programs tailored to gifted children. Miguel's journey became a community effort, with neighbors and mentors pitching in to provide guidance and support. This collective approach opened doors to opportunities previously out of reach. As a result, Miguel flourished academically and developed a keen sense of belonging and gratitude for the community that rallied around him.

In a different part of town, the Nguyen family faced the challenge of supporting their twice-exceptional son, Kai. Being from an underrepresented group added another layer of complexity to their situation. Initially, Kai's school misunderstood his unique needs, mistaking his learning challenges as disinterest. Frustrated but resolute, the Nguyens collaborated tirelessly with educators to help them recognize Kai's dual needs. They collaborated to create a customized education plan emphasizing academic growth and emotional support. This comprehensive approach, aligned with federal mandates for addressing all educational needs, transformed Kai's school experience. He began to excel academically, and his emotional well-being improved as he finally received support. The Nguyen family's determination and advocacy highlight the importance of recognizing and addressing the unique challenges twice-exceptional children from diverse backgrounds face.

Single-parent households often face unique challenges, as demonstrated by the story of Sarah, a single mom raising her gifted daughter, Emma. Balancing work, family responsibilities, and Emma's educational needs became overwhelming. Sarah knew she needed to manage her time more efficiently to support Emma's academic success. She built a robust support network, enlisting the help of community programs and online resources designed for gifted children. These became lifelines, providing Emma with the academic enrichment she craved. Despite the hurdles, Sarah's dedication ensured that Emma excelled in her studies and thrived emotionally. The success of this single-parent household serves as a reminder that, with the right strategies and support, even the most complex situations can yield remarkable outcomes.

We hope reading about these diverse experiences has enriched your understanding of nurturing gifted children. Each story illustrates the unique paths families traversed to support their children's extraordinary abilities. From cultural adaptations to socioeconomic hurdles, these narratives highlight the resilience and creativity of parents determined to provide the best for their children.

# EXPERT ADVICE AND ADDITIONAL RESOURCES

Parenting a gifted child can often feel overwhelmed due to the unique challenges it presents. However, you are not alone in this experience. This chapter provides insights from experienced parents who have successfully faced similar situations. It offers guidance and strategies to help you understand and support your gifted child's needs effectively.

Integrating expert insights into your parenting toolkit adds depth and credibility to your approach. Evidence-based strategies from seasoned psychologists and educators provide a roadmap, ensuring you are not wandering but moving purposefully. These professionals have dedicated their careers to understanding the complexities of giftedness, and their experiences bring invaluable perspectives to the table.

We'll begin with wisdom from a child psychologist specializing in gifted children. This expert will look at the common psychological challenges these kids often face, such as emotional roller coasters and perfectionism. They'll provide practical, insightful coping strategies, helping you turn those turbulent moments into opportunities for growth. You'll learn how to help your child channel their emotional intensity into creative outlets and teach them to embrace imperfections as steppingstones to success. We hope you'll find these strategies, grounded in research and real-world experience, helpful.

Next, we'll hear from an educational specialist who breathes life into individualized learning plans. This expert will share strategies for crafting educational experiences tailored to your child's unique needs, ensuring their academic journey is as enriching as it is challenging. They'll offer advice on advocating for your child's needs within the educational system, a daunting task for many. With their advice, you will learn to balance academic rigor with emotional support, creating an environment where your child can thrive without feeling overwhelmed. This is about helping your child flourish academically and emotionally during their school years.

However, wisdom comes not just from the professionals but also from the trenches of everyday life. We'll sit down with a parent who has successfully maneuvered through the challenges of raising a gifted child. Their real-life coping strategies offer a relatable and practical perspective, showing how they supported their child's academic and emotional needs. This parent shares about how to build a supportive family environment that encourages open communication and mutual respect. They also emphasize finding a community and support network, reminding us that raising a gifted child is a team effort, not a solo mission. Their journey is a testament to the power of resilience, adaptability, and the importance of leaning on others for support and guidance.

*Interactive Element: Reflection Exercise*

Take a moment to reflect on your journey so far as a parent of a gifted child. What challenges have you faced and what strategies have proven effective? Write down your thoughts and experiences and think about how the insights shared in this chapter might apply to your unique situation. This reflection can nourish your personal growth and remind you that you are not alone.

## 12.1 SITTING DOWN WITH SEASONED EXPLORERS

**Pearls of Wisdom from a Child Psychologist**

Gifted children often live in a world of heightened emotions and intense perceptions. According to Dr. Elaine Morgan, a child psychologist specializing in gifted children, this intensity can manifest in emotional roller coasters that overwhelm parents and children alike. Dr. Morgan emphasizes understanding and validating these emotions is the first step in navigating them. She explains, "Gifted children experience the world in high definition. Their joys are brighter, their fears are darker, and their frustrations can feel insurmountable. Our role is to help them see these emotions not as obstacles but as part of their unique brilliance."

One of the most common challenges faced by gifted children is perfectionism. This "beast," as Dr. Morgan calls it, can paralyze them with fear of failure. To combat this, she suggests strategies such as setting realistic goals, celebrating effort over outcomes, and modeling healthy self-compassion. For example, teaching your child to reframe mistakes as opportunities to learn can transform moments of frustration into growth.

Dr. Morgan also highlights the importance of channeling emotional intensity into creative outlets. Whether through art, music, writing, or physical activity, these outlets allow children to process their feelings constructively. She provides practical exercises like keeping a "feelings journal" or engaging in mindfulness activities to help them manage overwhelming emotions. "When children learn to navigate their emotions," Dr. Morgan adds, "they grow stronger and unlock new depths of creativity and problem-solving skills."

### Crafting Individualized Learning Plans: Insights from an Educational Specialist

Every gifted child's learning journey is unique, requiring an educational plan tailored to their strengths and challenges. Educational specialist Dr. Rachel Lin explains that individualized learning plans (ILPs) ensure gifted children thrive academically. "The key is to see the child as a whole," Dr. Lin advises, "not just as a student excelling in math or reading, but as a young person with emotional, social, and intellectual needs."

Dr. Lin advocates collaboration between parents, teachers, and administrators when crafting an ILP. She recommends a comprehensive assessment of your child's abilities and interests. From there, parents can work with educators to design a plan incorporating enrichment activities, advanced coursework, or opportunities for independent study. For example, a child passionate about astronomy might benefit from a mentorship with a local astronomer or participation in a science competition.

Advocating for your child within the educational system can feel like navigating a labyrinth. Dr. Lin encourages parents to approach these conversations as a partnership, bringing data and specific examples of their child's needs. She also stresses the importance of balancing academic rigor with emotional support. "Gifted children often face immense pressure to perform," she explains. "Ensuring they have a safe space to decompress and recharge is just as important as challenging their intellect."

### Lessons from the Trenches: A Parent's Perspective

While professionals provide invaluable guidance, nothing compares to the wisdom gained from lived experience. Lisa Martinez, a mother of two gifted children, shares her journey of raising children as emotionally complex as intellectually advanced.

Lisa recalls how she initially struggled to find the right balance between pushing her children to reach their potential and giving them the freedom to be kids. "I learned that it's okay to let them fail sometimes," she says. "Failure is where resilience is built, which carries them through life's challenges."

One of Lisa's key strategies was creating a supportive family environment where open communication and mutual respect were paramount. Family meetings became regular in her household, allowing everyone to share their thoughts and feelings. This approach strengthened family bonds and taught her children the value of empathy and teamwork.

Lisa also emphasizes the importance of finding a community of like-minded parents. Joining local support groups and online forums for parents of gifted children gave her access to resources, advice, and a sense of solidarity. "Raising a gifted child isn't something you can do alone," she says. "Having a network of people who understand your challenges makes all the difference."

## 12.2 RECOMMENDED BOOKS AND WEBSITES

When knee-deep in raising a gifted child, sometimes you may long for information but aren't sure where to find it. The good news is that a treasure trove of books exists, offering a great deal of wisdom and support. These reads cover everything from emotional and psychological development to educational resources and guides, not forgetting the all-important parenting strategies and support for managing the unique needs of gifted children. A standout is *A Parent's Guide to Gifted Children* by James Webb *et al.* This book looks at peer relations, motivation, discipline, and educational planning.

Another gem is *Emotional Intensity in Gifted Students* by Christine Fonseca, which tackles those big feelings with grace, offering strategies to help manage the emotional intensity that can sometimes accompany intellectual brilliance.

Then there's *Smart but Scattered* by Peg Dawson and Richard Guare, which focuses on assisting children to develop executive skills.

In our digital age, where information is but a click away, educational websites have become a beacon for parents seeking guidance. The National Association for Gifted Children (NAGC) is a wonderful resource, offering everything from academic articles to impactful research and advocacy.

Another invaluable site is the Davidson Institute, which provides resources tailored to the gifted community, including articles, research, and forums for parents. For those evenings when you are pondering existential questions about your child's future, these websites can offer a sense of direction and a wealth of knowledge to tap into. But do not stop there! Websites like Khan Academy provide free and accessible online learning platforms and courses, turning your living room into a mini classroom where your child can explore subjects at their own pace.

Interactive online resources can transform learning from a chore into an adventure. Educational games and apps like Prodigy or Scratch offer a playful way to engage with math and coding. They are the modern-day equivalent of sneaking vegetables into your child's favorite dish—fun and educational without them even realizing it. Virtual museum tours, like those offered by the Louvre and the Smithsonian, allow your child to wander through the history and art halls from the comfort of home, sparking curiosity and imagination. Science experiments from sites like Science Buddies provide step-by-step guides that turn your home into a makeshift lab where hypotheses can be evaluated and theories brought to life. These resources can ignite a passion for learning that stretches beyond the walls of a traditional classroom, providing endless possibilities for exploration and discovery.

### *Interactive Element: Book Club for Parents*

Consider starting a book club with fellow parents of gifted children. Choose one of the recommended books each month and come together to discuss insights and strategies. This can be a terrific way to build a supportive community while gaining new perspectives on raising gifted children. Plus, it is a perfect excuse for a night out with like-minded adults who understand your world. Sharing experiences and exchanging ideas can provide the camaraderie and support that every parent needs on this remarkable journey of raising a gifted child.

## 12.3 SUPPORT GROUPS AND ORGANIZATIONS

Support groups can make all the difference when you need a helping hand or listening ear. These groups transform isolation into a shared adventure, providing emotional and practical support. Being part of a community where others understand your challenges can be a big relief. You can share experiences, swap advice, and sometimes vent about the chaos. They offer a safe space to discuss everything from your child's latest existential crisis to their newfound obsession with black holes without fear of judgment or bewildered looks.

Finding local support groups can be challenging but the rewards are worth it. Start by contacting your child's school or local community centers. These places often have bulletin boards or newsletters that list meetings of parent groups. You might also find success by searching online for groups that meet in your area. Websites and forums often have directories of local gatherings. If all else fails, channel your inner social butterfly and network with other parents. You never know who else might be looking for a community just like you. Sometimes, forming a new group with fellow parents can lead to lasting friendships and valuable support systems.

National and international organizations offer a wealth of resources for those who prefer a broader reach. The National Association for Gifted Children (NAGC) is a cornerstone for advocacy and support, providing resources and hosting events connecting parents and professionals. The Davidson Institute for Talent Development offers many programs and resources tailored to gifted children and their families. Supporting the Emotional Needs of the Gifted (SENG) is another resource for those focusing on emotional well-being, providing guidance and community for navigating the emotional landscapes often accompanying giftedness. These organizations are like the wise elders of the gifted community, offering advice and support from a wealth of experience.

In this digital age, online support communities are virtual campfires where parents gather to share stories and strategies. Facebook groups dedicated to parents of gifted children can provide real-time support and a sense of belonging. These groups are often moderated by experienced parents or educators who can offer insights and advice. Online forums and discussion boards, like those found on the Davidson Institute's website, allow for more in-depth conversations about specific challenges and triumphs. Virtual support groups and webinars offer opportunities to connect with others in a more structured format, often led by professionals in the field.

### *Visual Element: Infographic on Support Group Benefits*

Try creating an infographic that outlines the benefits of joining a support group. Include statistics on parental stress reduction, increased access to resources, and the sense of community and belonging that these groups provide. This visual can serve as a motivating reminder of the support available to you and the positive impact it can have on your family's journey with giftedness.

Connecting with support groups and organizations transforms the often-solitary path of raising a gifted child into a shared experience rich with camaraderie and understanding. These connections provide immediate relief and equip you with the means and confidence to support your talented child effectively.

## 12.4 CONTINUING YOUR JOURNEY: LIFELONG SUPPORT AND LEARNING

Parenting a gifted child is not a sprint but a marathon, and as any seasoned runner will tell you, the key is pacing yourself and staying informed. In this ever-evolving landscape, lifelong learning is essential, not just for your child but for you as well. As your child's needs change, so must your strategies. What worked last year might not cut it now, so you need to stay updated on the latest research and resources. New educational methods, psychological insights, and technological advancements can offer fresh perspectives and solutions, so staying informed is more than just beneficial—it is necessary.

For those of you looking to continue your own education, there are plenty of avenues to explore. Attending workshops and conferences on gifted education can be a notable change. They provide knowledge and the opportunity to connect with experts and parents who share your experiences. Online courses or certification programs can fit seamlessly into your busy schedule, offering a flexible way to dive deeper into topics that matter most to you and your child. The latest research and publications keep you abreast of new gifted education and parenting strategies developments.

Engaging in lifelong learning with your child makes education a shared experience. Exploring new subjects and hobbies together can be a fantastic bonding experience. Whether learning a new language, picking up an instrument, or learning about the Amazon jungle, these activities can ignite a shared passion for discovery. Participating in educational events and activities as a family reinforces the value of learning and provides cherished memories.

This chapter has highlighted the importance of lifelong learning and dedicated support networks. Adaptation and continuous growth are essential to successfully supporting your gifted child. By staying informed and connected, you ensure you and your child are well-prepared for the future.

# CONCLUSION

As we reach the end of our journey together, let's take a moment to revisit the path we have traveled. This book is intended to be your trusty guide through the exhilarating, albeit occasionally bewildering, world of parenting a gifted child. I have aimed to equip you with actionable strategies, insights, resources, and support to help unlock your child's potential, grow their emotional resilience, and traverse those sometimes-perplexing educational systems.

The key takeaway from this book is that parenting a gifted child is a unique challenge and a remarkable opportunity. It is a difficult journey, but armed with the right strategies and support, you can guide your child to lifelong success and fulfillment.

I encourage you to reflect on the information and strategies we have shared. Consider how they apply to your unique family situation. Take a moment to think about the changes you can make today to support your gifted child better. Remember, every small step counts and can make a significant difference in your child's life.

Now, I invite you to act. Whether it is reaching out to your child's school to discuss acceleration options, setting up a calming space for mindfulness practices, or simply celebrating your child's unique talents, take that next step.

Lastly, I want to express my deepest gratitude to you. Thank you for your dedication, willingness to learn, and unwavering commitment to nurturing your child's brilliance. It has been an honor to walk this path with you. I hope this book serves as a steadfast companion in your ongoing journey.

# MAKE A DIFFERENCE!

As your child's abilities continue to amaze and challenge you, I doubt you'll find even more ways to support them. This is your starting kit; now, you can share it with more parents.

By sharing your honest opinion of this book and how it's helped you, you'll show new readers where they can find all the same guidance, they need to support their gifted children. Please leave a review now.

**Thank you so much for your support. You're making a big difference.**

# REFERENCES

Davidson Institute. (n.d.). The 6 different types of gifted students. https://www.davidsongifted.org/gifted-blog/profiles-of-the-gifted-and-talented/

Raising Lifelong Learners. (n.d.). Asynchronous development in gifted children. https://raisinglifelonglearners.com/asynchronous-development/

Raising Lifelong Learners. (n.d.). Overexcitabilities and why they matter for gifted kids. https://raisinglifelonglearners.com/overexcitabilities-and-why-they-matter-for-gifted-kids/

ERIC. (2018). Strategies for supporting students who are twice-exceptional. https://files.eric.ed.gov/fulltext/EJ1185416.pdf

Davidson Institute. (n.d.). Emotional intensity in gifted children. https://www.davidsongifted.org/gifted-blog/emotional-intensity-in-gifted-children/

Big Life Journal. (n.d.). 7 ways to help your child with perfectionism. https://biglifejournal.com/blogs/blog/help-child-with-perfectionism

Supporting Emotional Needs of the Gifted (SENG). (n.d.). Fortifying emotional resilience in gifted students. https://www.sengifted.org/post/fortifying-emotional-resilience-in-gifted-students

Supporting Emotional Needs of the Gifted (SENG). (n.d.). Combating under-achievement in gifted students through social-emotional training and development. https://www.sengifted.org/post/combating-underachievement-in-gifted-students-through-social-emotional-training-and-development

Study.com. (n.d.). Teaching communication skills to gifted students. https://study.com/academy/lesson/teaching-communication-skills-to-gifted-students.html

Positive Psychology. (n.d.). Positive reinforcement for kids: 11+ examples for parents. https://positivepsychology.com/parenting-positive-reinforcement/

Ascend Psychology. (n.d.). Creating a stimulating learning environment at home for gifted children. https://www.ascendpsychology.com/post/creating-a-stimulating-learning-environment-at-home-for-gifted-children

Parenting Bright Minds. (n.d.). The gifted child's guide to time management. https://parentingbrightminds.com/The-Gifted-Childs-Guide-to-Time-Management/

Vanguard Gifted Academy. (n.d.). Gifted education: Unveiling the pros and cons. https://vanguardgiftedacademy.org/latest-news/gifted-education-unveiling-the-pros-and-cons

Trépanier, C. (2017, March 28). The benefits of homeschooling gifted children. https://tiltparenting.com/2017/03/28/homeschooing-gifted-children/

Davidson Institute. (n.d.). Gifted education: Options for gifted students. https://www.davidsongifted.org/prospective-families/gifted-education-and-support-options/

Parent's Unofficial Guide to Gifted IEPs and GIEP Meetings. (n.d.). http://pvpage.wdfiles.com/local--files/resources/Parents_Unofficial_Guide_to_Gifted_IEPs_and_G.pdf

Davidson Institute. (n.d.). Highly gifted children and peer relationships. https://www.davidsongifted.org/gifted-blog/highly-gifted-children-and-peer-relationships/

InfoAge Publishing. (n.d.). Identifying, preventing, and combating bullying in gifted education. https://www.infoagepub.com/products/Identifying-Preventing-and-Combating-Bullying-in-Gifted-Education

We Are Teachers. (n.d.). 43 awesome team-building activities for kids. https://www.weareteachers.com/team-building-games-and-activities/

National Association for the Education of Young Children (NAEYC). (2017, March). Teaching emotional intelligence in early childhood. https://www.naeyc.org/resources/pubs/yc/mar2017/teaching-emotional-intelligence

University of Texas at Austin. (n.d.). How to teach: Divergent thinking. https://ctl.utexas.edu/sites/default/files/TeachingGuide_HowtoTeachDivergentThinking.pdf

BC Parent. (n.d.). 5 tips on how to be more Socratic with your children. https://bcparent.ca/socratic-method/

Create Inspire Teach. (2023, February 21). Enrichment activities for gifted learners. https://createinspireteach.com/2023/02/21/enrichment-activities/

University of Connecticut. (2023, May). Using investigative learning to develop high potentials. https://gifted.uconn.edu/wp-content/uploads/sites/961/2023/05/Freedom-to-Teach.pdf

ERIC. (2021). Managing the emotional intensities of gifted students with neurodiverse strategies. https://files.eric.ed.gov/fulltext/EJ1321310.pdf

Times of India. (2023, September 12). Regular exercise can reduce stress in school children, new study finds. https://timesofindia.indiatimes.com/life-style/parenting/moments/regular-exercise-can-reduce-stress-in-school-children-new-study-finds/articleshow/103580254.cms

Verywell Mind. (n.d.). Gifted kid burnout: Signs and how to overcome it. https://www.verywellmind.com/gifted-kid-burnout-signs-symptoms-how-to-overcome-it-8611238

South Carolina Department of Education. (n.d.). Gifted and talented support services. https://ed.sc.gov/instruction/standards-learning/advanced-academic-programs/gifted-and-talented/gifted-and-talented-support-services/

Free Spirit Publishing Blog. (n.d.). SMART goals for gifted students. https://blog. freespiritpublishing.com/smart-goals-for-gifted-students

Mindset Works. (n.d.). How parents can instill a growth mindset at home. https:// www.mindsetworks.com/parents/growth-mindset-parenting

Gifted Challenges. (2020, September). Ten college planning tips: What families of gifted children need to know. https://giftedchallenges.blogspot.com/2020/09/ ten-college-planning-tips-what-families.html

iLEAD Schools. (n.d.). Nurturing lifelong learners: Cultivating a love for learning in your child. https://ileadschools.org/nurturing-lifelong-learners-cultivating-a-love-for-learning-in-your-child/

Mutual of Omaha. (n.d.). Financial planning for your kid's education. https://www. mutualofomaha.com/advice/tackle-my-finances/tips-to-plan-for-your-chil drens-education-without-sacrificing-your-financial-goals

Davidson Institute. (n.d.). List of scholarships for younger students. https://www. davidsongifted.org/gifted-blog/list-of-scholarships-for-younger-students/

Davidson Institute. (n.d.). Twelve cost-effective educational options for serving gifted students. https://www.davidsongifted.org/gifted-blog/twelve-cost-effec tive-educational-options-for-serving-gifted-students/

Davidson Institute. (n.d.). Resources for gifted children & their families. https:// www.davidsongifted.org/resource-library/

Asana. (n.d.). The Eisenhower Matrix: How to prioritize your to-do list. https:// asana.com/resources/eisenhower-matrix

National Association for Gifted Children. (n.d.). https://nagc.org/

MGH Clay Center. (n.d.). 10 self-care tips for parents. https://www.mghclaycenter. org/parenting-concerns/10-self-care-tips-for-parents/

Anchor Light Therapy. (n.d.). 10 healthy family communication skills & how to implement them. https://anchorlighttherapy.com/family-communication/

Davidson Institute for Talent Development. (n.d.). Successful advocacy for gifted students. http://print.ditd.org/EdGuild_PowerPoints/EdGuild_Successful_Ad vocacy_for_Gifted_Students.pdf

Woodsmall Law Group. (n.d.). Securing education for your twice-exceptional student. https://www.woodsmalllawgroup.com/parent-resources/secure-educa tion-for-2e-student/

Simple Homeschool. (n.d.). Homeschooling my gifted child: Here's why it was the best choice. https://simplehomeschool.net/homeschooling-my-gifted-child/

ERIC. (n.d.). Affirming culturally different gifted students. https://files.eric.ed.gov/ fulltext/EJ874024.pdf

SENG. (n.d.). An interview with Dr. Tracy Cross: The social and emotional needs of gifted children. https://www.sengifted.org/post/an-interview-with-dr-tracy-cross-the-social-and-emotional-needs-of-gifted-children

Davidson Institute. (n.d.). Gifted 101: Our favorite gifted parenting books. https://www.davidsongifted.org/gifted-blog/gifted-101-our-favorite-gifted-parenting-books/

Supporting Emotional Needs of the Gifted (SENG). (n.d.). SENG | Community groups. https://www.sengifted.org/scg